Does My Dog Love Me?

Also by Graeme Hall

All Dogs Great and Small
Perfectly Imperfect Puppy

Does My Dog Love Me?

Understanding How Your Dog Sees the World

Graeme Hall

EBURY
SPOTLIGHT

1

Ebury Spotlight, an imprint of Ebury Publishing
20 Vauxhall Bridge Road
London SW1V 2SA

Ebury Spotlight is part of the Penguin Random House group of companies
whose addresses can be found at global.penguinrandomhouse.com

First published by Ebury Spotlight in 2024

www.penguin.co.uk

A CIP catalogue record for this book is available from the British Library

ISBN 9781529149234

Typeset in 11.75/17.9pt SabonNext LT Regular by Jouve (UK), Milton Keynes
Printed and bound in Great Britain by Clays Ltd, Elcograf S.p.A.

The authorised representative in the EEA is Penguin Random House Ireland,
Morrison Chambers, 32 Nassau Street, Dublin D02 YH68

Penguin Random House is committed to a
sustainable future for our business, our readers
and our planet. This book is made from Forest
Stewardship Council® certified paper.

To Nikki, much loved by dogs,
horses and a Yorkshireman.

Contents

Contents

Prologue

'Does my dog love me?' is a very human question to ask – doesn't everyone want to know that they're loved? – but impossible to answer succinctly.

You could ask 20 people what love means and get 20 different responses. Philosophers, poets, playwrights and novelists have been wrestling with the nature of love for centuries, while pop musicians have been trying to get to the bottom of it for the best part of 75 years. Just think of all those famous hits: 'I Want to Know What Love Is', 'Have You Ever Been in Love', 'Is This Love', 'What Is Love'. What chance do dogs have of fathoming it out?

Some more hopeful souls believe science might one day be able to tell us, categorically, if our dogs love us. As it is, research has shown that dogs are drawn to people pretending to cry, and that the relevant part of a dog's brain responds more emphatically to human praise than to food. But maybe the most compelling evidence of doggy love comes from their urine (aah, the romance.)

When scientists analysed dog and human wee, they found that both species release oxytocin, the so-called 'love hormone', when they look at each other (the same thing happens in humans when they're cradling babies and hugging). Remember that the next time your dog goes to the toilet on the living room floor – maybe he's trying to tell you he loves you … Bless him.

The bottom line is, we don't know for sure if dogs love their owners, because you can't sit down with a dog and pour your heart out with a pot of tea and a plate of custard creams. And, let's face it, that day will probably never come.

An easier question to answer is: do dogs feel emotions? If so, are they the same emotions as ours? Again, dogs can't tell us what they feel, but certain emotions are easier to decipher than something as nebulous as love, which even the most intelligent humans find difficult to pin down.

Almost everything we know about dogs is based on what we can observe, whether by owners or by academics in places of learning. Put simply, people try to work out what's going on in a dog's head by how they're acting, in much the same way as adult humans try to work out what's going on in children's heads before they're able to verbally communicate their feelings.

Humans have a tendency to anthropomorphise animals – in other words, attribute human traits, emotions and intentions to them (Walt Disney has a lot to answer for!). Without meaning to sound harsh to dogs, sometimes we give them a little too much credit. Yes, dogs are smart compared to most animals, but they're not people, in that their thinking simply isn't as sophisticated. At least not in a human sense.

For example, people often get a dog when they're grieving for someone and are feeling lonely, because they believe it will be a direct replacement. That's putting a lot of pressure on that dog, because dogs don't see the world quite like us. But in other ways, we don't anthropomorphise dogs enough.

For years, dog trainers tended to say, 'Humans are humans, dogs are dogs', and focused on the differences. Dare I say, there was perhaps a hint of 'We've got these special magical powers that non-dog trainers couldn't possibly understand.' Sure, there are differences, but I've come to believe that there's something like an 80 per cent overlap between basic human and dog behaviour. As the years pass, there's more and more science behind that premise. As such, sometimes we could understand dogs a lot better if we spent more time comparing them to humans and asking the question, 'Right, what would *we* be thinking in this situation?' In other words, sometimes we get in trouble by over-anthropomorphising, and other times, the opposite.

* * *

If this is beginning to sound like a bit of a cop-out ('I bought a book called *Does My Dog Love Me?* and he tells us on page one he's not going to answer it'), let me explain: in this book I've set out to tackle this and many other tricky dog questions that, experience has taught me, owners want to know. The truth is that for most of them, there simply isn't a black-and-white yes/ no answer. It takes a book to answer them. But this isn't just a book about doggy emotions, it's also a book about how dogs perceive and navigate the world, what makes them tick, why they do what they do, and how much they understand us. Or don't, as the case may be.

In the following pages, I'll use all my experience as a dog trainer, a job I've been doing for 15 years and counting, taking in more than 5,000 dogs and quite a few series of my TV show

Dogs Behaving (Very) Badly, to help you fix problems, bring you and your dog even closer and make everyone involved, man and dog, happier. Any dog, any age, any problem – that's my motto.

As well as a stack of personal stories, from the sublime to the ridiculous and everything in between, I'll delve into research by some of the world's finest canine scientists and behaviourists. You'll be amazed by some of the things they've uncovered. To be completely honest, so was I!

Anyway, back to love. Recently, I went to see a guy who had a two-year-old Labrador called Larry. This guy was really quite upset, despite Larry's problems seeming fairly standard, such as getting distracted by things in the park and pulling on the lead.

Most of the problems occurred outside, so off we went for a walk on Wimbledon Common. Sure enough, after about an hour Larry spotted some squirrels and started pulling. But even after we'd fixed that problem, which didn't take long, the owner still seemed quite perturbed.

When I asked what was wrong, he told me that Larry also had a problem with recall. And when we started chucking a ball about, I realised that the one thing Larry loved more than a ball was people. So while he did bring the ball back to his owner occasionally, he'd often barrel across the Common to get strangers to throw it for him – 'You throw my ball! Now you throw my ball!'

This wasn't a difficult fix either, because a Labrador and food are a match made in heaven. All the owner had to do was rustle a bag of treats and Larry would come back lively. But whenever he did so, the owner would get emotional. Now, I'm used to seeing people happy and excited when something starts to work, or disappointed if it doesn't – I see a whole spectrum of emotions on a daily basis in my work – but this was unusual and unexpected. This was tears-welling-up, lump-in-the-throat emotion. When I asked if he was okay, he replied, 'Yeah, all I ever wanted was for him to love me.'

That's when the penny dropped: the owner thought Larry wanting to play with other people meant he didn't love him, or didn't think he was enough. That's a common feeling among dog owners, and ties in with what I was saying about love being a nebulous, and very human, concept.

Still, people feel love from their dogs in many different ways. Others, being more pragmatic, might not feel love at all. They accept that their dog needs them, rather than loves them, while not loving their dog any less because of it. But – and here's the crux – does it really matter if our dogs love us or not? Does it really matter if our dogs view our co-habitation as a marriage of convenience? Surely all that matters is that we love them? For the record, I don't need any scientific evidence, I have blind faith that my dogs love me. And I *know* I love them. What else matters, really?

As for you, dear reader, by the end of this book, hopefully you'll understand your dog better, which will make the bond between you even stronger. And maybe you'll be closer to knowing whether your dog loves you or not. Like dogs, we're all individuals. And if you do choose to believe, who am I to judge?

Chapter 1

How Human Are Dogs?

Dogs were the first animals to be domesticated by humans, that much we know. I'll return to how they came to be domesticated later in the book, but we know they were around at the time of the first human settlements in the Mediterranean, around 11,000 years ago, because their remains have been found buried alongside their human masters, and there are even earlier examples that have been found elsewhere. (Modern cats are relative Johnny-come-latelies, incidentally, having arrived on the scene about 7,000 years later.)

As such, dogs, like no other species, have evolved to fit in with human society. They guard us, help us hunt, sit on our laps, sleep in our beds and lick our faces when we're feeling a bit down in the dumps. But here's the weird thing: while generations of humans claimed to know what their dogs were thinking, they were really just guessing.

Only in recent years, with the rise of canine cognitive science as a serious discipline, have scientists turned to more sophisticated methods and delved deeper into dogs' behaviour. As a result, we're beginning to understand exactly what's going on between a dog's ears and how like us they really are.

A 2017 study by Princeton University found that hyper-social dogs carry variants of certain genes – the same variants that can be seen in humans who have a rare genetic disorder called Williams-Beuren syndrome, a key feature of which is hyper-sociality. The researchers speculated that the more time wolves (or proto-dogs) spent with humans, the more those genes related to sociality were boosted. If that really is what happened, we can reasonably say, at least in this respect, dogs are evolving to become more like humans.

While dog brains are smaller than human brains, they are strikingly similar in terms of structure, which suggests they work along the same lines. For example, dogs have a hippo-campus, because they need to remember things, and they have an amygdala, because they get aroused, excited and scared.

Dr Gregory Berns of Emory University in Atlanta has trained dozens of dogs to voluntarily walk into a functional magnetic resonance imaging (fMRI) scanner, place their heads on a chin rest and lay down, stock-still, for 15 to 20 minutes while their brains are being scanned (if the dogs were restrained or sedated, their brains would behave differently). I take my hat off to the trainers who achieved this. Dr Berns's research has shown that areas of the human brain that are active when experiencing certain emotions are also active in canine brains, which may suggest that dogs experience similar emotions to us. That's pretty astonishing stuff, I'm sure you'll agree.

So while dogs aren't going to be running the country any time soon (more's the pity, some would argue), they're a lot more 'human' than you might have thought.

Do dogs get lonely?

When I was filming *Dogs Behaving (Very) Badly Australia* in 2023, Covid lockdowns were almost a taboo subject, probably because Australia had some of the strictest lockdown rules in the world. I'd say to owners, 'I think your dog's issues are partly due to lockdown,' and they'd reply, 'Do we have to talk about that? We want to forget all about it . . .'

But the honest truth is, we already had a generation of dogs purchased during Covid that were a bit unhinged, because of a lack of socialisation (according to the Pet Food Manufacturers' Association, 3.2 million UK households acquired a new pet in the first year of the pandemic, many of them dogs). Then when Covid abated, owners returned to work – unless you were one of the lucky ones allowed to carry on working from home – so now you had poorly socialised dogs who were being left on their own, probably thinking, 'My owners haven't been out of my sight for months on end, and now they're nowhere to be seen for hours on end.' No wonder they were confused.

Suddenly, I was hearing a lot of stories about dogs barking, crying and howling the house down, hiding in strange places, and chewing through doors and sofas. And those are all classic signs of separation anxiety.

Sometimes, what appears to be separation anxiety – otherwise known as monophobia, or fear of being alone – isn't that at all. Dogs can cause damage because they're bored, or they'll bark at passersby because they're nervous. Or maybe they're just acting up as you leave, but as soon as you get in the car and go, they calm down and go back to bed until you get home.

Actual separation anxiety can be very distressing, for everyone involved. One lady sent me a phone video of her beagle, who was barking, howling and crying for hours, often while sitting on the sofa, looking out of the window. He was also scratching at every potential exit: the poor dog was literally trying to find a way out and bring his owner back.

This lady with the beagle had tried all sorts of things to calm her dog down, including leaving treats and sticking on some classical music. That was a nice idea, but Rachmaninoff's Piano Concerto No. 2, lovely as it is, was unlikely to be enough to fix separation anxiety, because the dog was still on his own.

Part of the solution can sometimes be giving your dog less room. If your dog has the whole house to themselves, that's just space to zoom around in and wind themselves up. But if you create a small, cosy area at the back of the house, where it's quieter, your dog will hopefully see it as a den, a little pocket of tranquillity and safety. You could also leave something in the den to occupy their brain, such as a puzzle or a rubber toy with some treats inside.

Ironically, for other dogs, the feeling of being cooped up can be at the root of the problem. Rescue dogs in particular often rage against being held captive in a crate – no doubt it brings back bad memories – and will go to extraordinary lengths to escape. For them, giving them a free run of a room or two can make all the difference.

Unfortunately, it's not always as simple as working out how much space your dog needs, and fixing separation anxiety can take a lot of time and patience. I'd noticed from the beagle's phone video footage that he wasn't creating noise all the time; he'd stop occasionally, which was him listening. So I told his owner to pop out of the front door and pop back in just a few seconds later, but only in one of those short gaps when the dog had stopped creating (otherwise, the dog would think that he was responsible for bringing her back ... by barking!). During that short gap, the owner needed to get the treats and praise in, using a very calm voice, like you'd use to get a baby off to sleep, or if you were a radio DJ on a graveyard shift.

Over the next few days and possibly weeks, the lady needed to extend the amount of time between leaving and coming back, always matching her return with her dog's quiet moments. Eventually, the dog would make the connection between being quiet and her coming back, armed with tasty treats and lots of praise. And hopefully, it would reach the stage where the lady could be out of the house for a few hours without worrying about the neighbours. Or her dog worrying too, importantly.

A quick word on praise while we're on the subject. Praise is great, but you can overdo it. Think of the boss or old teacher who praised everything you did – chances are, it ended up meaning nothing, because it was so easily earned. But you might also have had a boss or teacher who only praised you every now and again, and when it came, it really meant something. It's the same with dogs. It's good to start out with lots of praise, so that they know they're on the right track, but slowly wean them off it. If you're always telling them what a good boy/girl they are, it will end up meaning nothing – but if you say it sparingly, they'll know they've done something really good when you do praise them.

A lady once called me to say she'd just rehomed a dog which was showing worrying signs of separation anxiety. She'd taken the first week off work, but on her second day back, she'd returned home at lunchtime to find her dog had eaten through a plasterboard wall, exposing wiring and plumbing.

When I visited this lady and her dog, it was immediately obvious that it was a classic case of separation anxiety, because the wall he'd eaten through was right next to the front door, through which he'd seen his owner leave.

The owner was at the end of her tether. She'd already used up all her holiday, and when she'd tried putting her dog in a crate, he'd broken out. Incredibly, he'd managed to bend the metal bars, making his paws bleed.

The lady explained that the dog was a rescue and that his previous foster owners had other dogs, which meant he was never on his own and, as a result, never anxious. On top of that, the foster carers had told the lady they'd gladly have the dog back permanently (to a home with many dogs where he'd never shown signs of separation anxiety) if it didn't work out with her. When she told me that, I said, 'I could give you loads of advice on how to deal with separation anxiety, but there are no quick fixes. And the longer you're together, the harder the bond is going to be to break. Actually, I think the perfect solution is staring us both in the face. There's another dog for you, there's another home for this dog, and you'll both be a lot happier if you go your separate ways.'

As an aside, separation anxiety is a good example of ingrained personality traits. I've seen webcam footage of two dogs in a house where one is going bananas and the other one is lying down, looking totally relaxed and looking at his mate as if to say, 'What the hell is his problem?' That said, if you already have a dog with separation anxiety, my advice is not to get another one in the hope it will solve the situation. You might get lucky, but you might not. In the worst-case scenario, you'll end up with two dogs with separation anxiety, because the new one will learn that behaviour from your old one.

* * *

Thankfully, I'm hearing about fewer Covid-related separation anxiety cases recently, and one reason for that is the proliferation of doggy daycare facilities and dogwalkers, which have popped up all over the country to offset the sudden absence of owners (go back a couple of decades and professional dogwalkers were almost unheard of).

I'm a big fan of doggy daycare, because it's a great way of teaching dogs how to interact harmoniously with other dogs – although I don't recommend sending your dog along if he's out of control and wants to do damage to other dogs. Daycare staff aren't trainers, so they won't thank you for that!

There's also been an explosion in the number of secure dog fields, which will charge you a modest amount to let your dog run around for an hour. They're a very simple idea but very handy, because most parks aren't dog-proofed, so there's always the worry your dog might leg it and end up on a dual carriageway.

They're especially useful if you've got a dog whose recall is poor or non-existent, or one who's what's known as 'reactive' because they overreact to certain stimuli, for example by growling, barking or lunging. A reactive dog is not to be confused with an aggressive dog, although it's sometimes difficult for strangers to tell.

At the high-tech end, a lot of people nowadays have webcams, like the lady with the dachshund, and gadgetry like that can be brilliant. I've met people who talk to their dogs while they're in the office, and even release treats for them. But tech can also make things worse if it's not used properly.

I've seen cases where owners thought their dog had a bit of a problem with a dog showing signs of anxiety when they left the house, so they rigged up a webcam, watched for a few days and convinced themselves it was a massive problem. Consequently, every time they left the house to go to work, they looked and sounded anxious themselves– 'Don't worry! Don't worry! I'll be back later!' – as if they were going off to war. Dogs pick up on that, and it can become a vicious circle, with the dog understandably going from perturbed to outright scared.

If you can talk to your dog remotely, think about your timing. If you can see they're anxious, it's only natural that you'll press the button and say, 'Good girl, everything's going to be all right', in your soppiest possible voice. The problem with that approach is the dog will be thinking, 'I'm barking and crying, and you're telling me I'm a good girl. Plus, you sound stressed out too. OK, I'll carry on doing it …'. Then there are the dogs who simply get spooked out by the ghostly sound of their owner's voice and lose the plot completely. Let's face it, you can't really blame them!

We're sending signals out and so precise timing is key. If you fancy giving a bit of kit like this a try, it's much better to wait for a moment when they settle down, then gently and calmly praise them for that instead. Whatever we reward – and praise is a great way to reward a dog – we encourage.

I should stress that there's nothing necessarily wrong with leaving your dog at home alone for three or four hours, because it won't bother some dogs in the slightest. In fact, most dogs will take themselves off to bed as soon as you've walked out the door, pleased that they've got some peace and quiet. I happily leave mine for four hours at a time. There is no magic number, it's just common sense, because one dog's five minutes alone can feel like another dog's five hours.

Do dogs cry?

Sometimes I'm asked, 'Is a dog's crying the same as a human's crying?' Depending on the situation, I think it can be. The other day, my better half took two of our dogs to the vet, after we'd all been out for a walk together. I went into the house with Jonny, who is about seven different breeds in one. I'd never seen him on his own, because we usually only take one dog to the vets at a time, and it didn't go down very well.

While I was upstairs making a few calls, he was downstairs whining and crying, and it's not as if I could say to him, 'Mate, you saw them go off in the Land Rover with Mum, they'll be back in a bit.' But what struck me most was that he was making a sound I'd not heard him make before, a very human kind of whining, and he even broke into a little bit of a howl at one point (not quite so human, admittedly!).

I wished I could say to him, 'Tell you what, come here and I'll give you a treat if you're quiet', but he wasn't interested in food anyway – even if I did get my timing right. I rather fancy he was thinking, 'How can I eat? I've come back in the house and the other two aren't here. This has never happened!' He calmed down eventually, bless him. (Perhaps because I was calm. At least that's what I'd like to think.)

Remarkably, a 2022 study by scientists from Azabu University in Japan suggested that a dog's eyes may well up with tears of happiness when they're reunited with their owner after a period apart. And the scientists speculated that those tears might have evolved to strengthen the dog–human bond.

We already knew that dogs have tear ducts to keep their eyes clean and healthy, but tears in dogs had never before been linked with emotion.

The lead scientist decided to launch the study after noticing that one of his dogs shed tears when she was nursing. Naturally, he wondered if his dog was overcome with happiness by the arrival of a litter of new puppies.

The experiment involved measuring the volume of tears shed by 18 dogs (they've got a special test for that) for a minute before and after they were reunited with their owners following five to seven hours of separation. Intriguingly, the quantity of tears shed went up by 10 per cent after they were reunited. However, tear volume didn't increase when they did the same experiment with dogs and people with whom they were just familiar.

The scientists suspected that oxytocin (often known as the 'love hormone' or 'maternal hormone' in humans) was at least partly responsible for producing the tears, so applied a solution containing oxytocin to the surface of another group of dogs' eyes. Hey presto, the volume of tears went up significantly.

As far as I'm aware, no research has been done on whether dogs shed tears in response to negative emotions, as humans do. We also don't know if tears play a role in inter-dog interactions. If it was found that they didn't, it would increase the possibility that dogs' emotional tear shedding evolved alongside domestication, in the same way as moveable eyebrows.

A 2019 Duke University study showed that dogs move their eyebrows far more often and with higher intensity than wolves do, with scientists hypothesising that dogs with expressive eyebrows, which produced 'puppy-dog eyes', triggered a nurturing response in humans. And the Japanese scientists thought it possible that a dog's teary eyes would do much the same. To test this theory, they showed 74 people pictures of dogs' faces with and without tears in them, and – surprise, surprise – it was the teary-eyed dogs that got the more positive responses.

Do dogs remember?

When dogs have a bit of a to-do, they don't hold a grudge. One minute, they'll be screaming at each other over a bone, the next they'll be curled up together on the same bed. Humans, in contrast, hold on to feelings, to the extent that one small, seemingly irrelevant spat can lead to two people never speaking to each other again for years. If ever. The world would be a better place if we were more like dogs in that respect.

Dogs do remember, just not in the same way as humans. So while your dog will hopefully remember hand signals and commands they were first taught at puppy training, and they might be able to lead you home from the train station, they're unlikely to remember the first time you met. Or even the last time.

A 2014 Swedish study suggested that dogs forget events within two minutes (which was actually a lot better than chimpanzees, human's closest living animal relative). That kind of memory of specific events is 'episodic', which is how you or I remember where we parked the car before shopping. Instead, dogs, like lots of other animals, have 'associative' memories, which means they store important information that will help them survive, like where to find food, or 'This is where someone stuck a needle in me ...' – what you might call a bad memory.

But just because your dog can't remember the last time you met – even though you only just popped out to the shop – that doesn't mean they don't remember who you are, which is why when you come back from the shop, they'll know you're not a stranger and carry on dozing. I'm also convinced that dogs can recognise people they haven't seen for years, although the memory may be more connected to sight and smell: 'Aaah, this person smells familiar ...'

It's tricky to study how long dogs remember people for, because that would involve separating them from their owners for long periods – how do you arrange that as part of an ethical academic experiment? – but there's piles of anecdotal evidence.

There's even a story in Homer's *Odyssey*, which is almost 3,000 years old: when Odysseus returns to his native land, after years of war and roaming, the first to recognise him is his dog Argos. Poor old Argos is just about strong enough to wag his tail but can't get up to greet his master, and Odysseus has to blank him, because he's in disguise. A tear rolls down Odysseus' cheek as he passes by, and Argos promptly dies. That's not the cheeriest tale (although it gets a lot worse), but it shows that humans have recognised dog memory for a long time.

Not so long ago, I read about a couple of beagles who were stolen from their owner in South Wales and found three years later in Berkshire, 200 miles away. When the happy chap picked his old mates up, they apparently went nuts, even though they were knocking on ten years old. I also read about a dog who ran away from her home in Texas, after being spooked by fireworks, and was found seven years later in Florida, 1,100 miles away. This poor dog could barely walk, but 'came to life at her owner's voice, licked his hand again and again, and inched her body as close as she could to him'. We don't know how that dog remembered who her owner was, but it was clear that she did, which is really quite lovely.

People are always saying to me, 'My dog was attacked by a crazed Mongolian ferret terrier*' – or some other breed – 'and it's been scared of that particular breed ever since.' Is it possible that a dog could have an issue with a particular breed? I've heard so many instances that I'm inclined to believe it, but only by association. Your dog is thinking, 'A dog that shape and size once hurt

---

* To save you a trip to Google, I should fess up here: no such breed exists outside of my imagination …

me/scared me.' That's subtly different to a human making a value judgement: 'Mongolian ferret terriers are bad dogs.' However, let's say your dog was nipped by a Border collie: it might just be coincidence that you've got a nervous dog and it's the fact Border collies run around at a thousand miles an hour that puts him on edge, not the fact that a Border collie once had a go at him.

Thankfully, you can change a dog's associative memory, which is where my training comes in. But you have to keep in mind something called 'temporal contiguity', which is the idea that for dogs to make an association, a behaviour and a stimulus must happen at the same time. Bear with me here because this is way easier to understand than that may sound. Here's an example: 'I bark and they give me treats, so I associate barking with treats.' It's not what their human had in mind when they were bribing the dog to be quiet, of course.

Note that connections are made between behaviours that humans consider 'good' or 'bad', and the stimulus could be positive (praise, treats etc.) or negative (a telling-off). As such, it's important not to tell your dog off after an event, because they won't make the connection. The classic example is toilet training: you come downstairs in the morning, your dog's had an accident in the hallway and your instinct is to chastise her. But she'll be thinking, 'Why is he annoyed? I'm sitting in the kitchen doing nothing.' It doesn't matter how much you point at her poo and get hot under the collar, she simply won't put the accident and your annoyance together because the action of going to the toilet and the eventual consequence happened at different times. In fact, the poor dog's most likely assuming she's in trouble for sitting quietly in the kitchen. Awww …

Similarly, if you walk in on your dog eating your best leather belt and you tell him off, or just give him a dirty look, he'll connect your displeasure with him eating the belt. But if you walk in and the belt is already in tatters on the floor, and your dog is looking pleased with himself and wagging his tail, job done, the moment has gone.

The problem with missing the moment is that your dog will connect the telling-off with what he's doing right now. So if you discover the belt in one room, march into another room where your dog is lounging on his bed and give him a few choice words, he'll assume that lounging on his bed is bad. That will be confusing, especially if you usually tell him what a good boy he is when you send him to it. He'll just think you're a bit weird, which can damage the bond between you. And ironically he still won't know that eating belts is less than endearing.

Sometimes, you have to try not to worry about what other people are thinking. Let's say you're in a café and your dog starts barking. You tell her to shush, she goes quiet and you say, 'Good girl,' and give her a treat. That's the right thing to do because your dog now associates barking with being naughty and being quiet with being good. But the people on the next table, who won't think like dogs, might wonder why you're rewarding your dog for barking. Do you know what? Let 'em. It's your dog you're teaching, not them.

Do dogs recognise their siblings?

There hasn't been much research into this topic, but one 1994 scent-based study by Queen's University Belfast determined that they weren't able to, at least after two years of separation (although dogs recognised their mothers and vice versa).

However, I think they sometimes might, because I've worked with thousands of dogs and heard lots of stories about two littermates meeting for the first time since they were separated and going bananas, in much the same way as two people who haven't seen each other for ages might do. I even saw it with my Rottweiler Axel: when he met one of his siblings, there was definitely a sense of, 'Yeah, there's something different about you …'

I recently saw a TV show about a litter of kelpies (Aussie sheepdogs) that was split up after eight weeks, with each dog being trained on a different farm. They checked in on the dogs after three, six and nine months, and the best-trained dog after 12 months was the winner. When they got them all back together for the first time since they were separated, a couple of them had a little spat, but that was soon forgotten about and there was definitely a sense that they all knew they were from the same litter. Of course, I might just be anthropomorphising (no one's perfect!), but it would be lovely if true.

Do dogs smile?

I've got a funny story about a 'smiling' dog. Years ago, I went on holiday to Australia and visited a friend of a friend who was having a few issues with his Dalmatian. When I turned up, the dog greeted me through the window, leaping up and baring his teeth frantically. But I knew right away that he wasn't being aggressive, that was just his way of saying hello. In fact, I'd describe the dog as smiling. If Cheshire cats smile, you can bet your bottom dollar Dalmatians do too.

Usually, we associate a dog baring their teeth with aggression, but you have to link it with what else is going on with their body. Dalmatians are one of those breeds who bare their teeth while widening their mouth and relaxing their lips. And their body isn't stiff when they do it, it's quite floppy.

When the guy turned up in his four-wheel drive, I told him about his dog's greeting and he said, 'Is there any way you can stop him doing that? It's become a real problem because I'll be on the other side of the estate and I'll get a phone call from a tradie telling me they can't go anywhere near the house, because my dog's threatening them through the window.' But as I suspected, when I got out of the car, he was as soft as tripe (but smelled better, thankfully). What I couldn't solve was how the guy was going to convince the tradesmen. I mean … would I even want him to stop smiling?

Do dogs get jealous?

Dogs' jealousy is different to ours. You won't find them cyber-stalking old flames on Facebook, or getting upset when they find out you've been cavorting with cavaliers, lounging with Labradors and playing with poodles. But they do show signs of a simple form of jealousy which is essentially a survival instinct.

There was quite a famous experiment done in the 1960s in which they separated human babies from their mums and then watched the babies' response when their mums started playing with lifelike baby dolls. Surprise, surprise, most of the babies cried, the inference being that that was the babies telling their mums, 'You've got the wrong one! It's me you need to feed!'

In 2021, researchers from the University of Auckland published the results of a similar experiment carried out with dogs and their owners. In the experiment, the owners interacted with a lifelike fake dog and, to cut a long story short, it didn't go down very well with the real dogs. The dogs would forcefully attempt to reach their owners, pulling on their leads far harder than when their owners were interacting with a fleece cylinder used as a control.

The researchers concluded that the dogs were displaying human-like jealous behaviour – like babies with their mums – which I found particularly intriguing, because when I first started out as a dog trainer, I was told, 'You mustn't anthropomorphise dogs, and there's no such thing as a jealous dog.' You may have heard similar.

But I'd always suspected jealousy in dogs existed – at least in some form – because owners kept on telling me about it. I'd hear about dogs who seemed jealous when a new dog was brought into the home, or a new human partner, or a new baby.

We don't know if some breeds are (or are perceived to be) more jealous than others, but I'd guess companion dogs are more likely to be jealous than working dogs, which is why my friend's Patterdale terrier couldn't care less when he gives attention to other dogs, while my other friend's Chihuahua goes nuts.

Sometimes, what looks like jealousy can be something else. Here's a story from years ago, but I've seen versions of it play out many times since. This couple I met had a Border collie, and every time they'd have a cuddle on the sofa, the dog would jump up and bark earnestly at them (anyone who's had a Border collie knows quite how piercing that bark can be!). Because he'd learnt his barking would immediately nip the affection in the bud, he wouldn't stop doing it and it was getting worse. But when I observed this dog's behaviour, I thought, 'That's not jealousy in a human sense, he's just being a bossy boots, because he wants attention from his mum and dad.' The solution involved giving him the attention and affection he craved only when he chose to be quiet. And because Border collies are smart, we managed to sort it out quickly.

People will often report that the only time their dog has ever bitten anyone is when he's guarding something he doesn't want them to have, which is known as resource guarding. The classic line is, 'My dog is normally a little angel and wouldn't hurt a fly, until he steals something, when he turns into a devil.'

When your dog is resource guarding, they will hunker down, often in their bed or the corner of the sofa, and their body language will say, 'Keep away from me. This thing is very valuable to me and you're not having it.'

Often there's a genetic element to it, and spaniels, among others, seem prone to indulge in a spot of resource guarding. I was playing with a cocker recently and she kept bringing a tennis ball to me and dropping it at my feet. But as soon as I put my hand down to pick it up, she'd snaffle it and run away. She was basically taunting me! That was a bit of fun, and it's not uncommon of course, but you can see how that kind of behaviour can morph into something more serious on rare occasions.

Sometimes resource guarding starts as attention seeking. The item doesn't actually mean that much to them, but they learn that if they nick something, all eyes will be on them. Dogs almost always show you what they've stolen in these cases, because chances are it will trigger a Keystone Cops pursuit all over the house, which is the best fun a dog can have. Then one day, it will go wrong. They'll back themselves into a corner, you'll try to take whatever it is off them, and they'll get scared and have a pop at you. You'll back off – understandably, because it can be quite shocking the first time it happens – and the dog has made the connection: 'Hang on a minute ... if I take this and run away, you'll try to take it back and scare me. I'll fight back, you'll go away, and I'll get to keep it.'

If it's a bone that your dog's guarding as if his life depended on it, the best advice is not to give your dog bones. (No apologies if that sounds like a cop-out, incidentally. Sometimes prevention really is better than a cure that risks injury and makes the problem worse.) But sometimes dogs will lash out and bite if they've got hold of absolutely anything – slippers, cushions, spectacles, socks, remote controls, I've heard it all. It's impossible to predict what your dog might decide to guard, and it can be quite difficult to fix the problem.

In many cases, the dog won't be destroying the item, they'll actually be guarding in quite a gentle way, which is the perfect segue into a near-disastrous situation I found myself in recently.

I was visiting a couple with a golden retriever who'd steal things and take them to a corner of the sofa. If anyone went near her, she'd growl. And if anyone tried to take the thing off her, she'd launch forwards and bite them, or at least try to.

While I was chatting to the owners about the case, I saw out of the corner of my eye that the dog had managed to open a cupboard door and had grabbed something. When it hit the floor, it burst open and a medical kit fell out, including some needles wrapped in cellophane. Quick as a flash, the dog grabbed them again, before scuttling back to her corner of the sofa. My career flashed in front of my eyes, and I thought she'd be on the operating table within the hour. This was one of the most delicate situations I'd ever found myself in, at least where dogs were concerned.

Any time I went near her, she started chomping on this packet of needles, as if to say, 'Don't come any closer, punk, or I'll swallow them.' So all I could do was wait and wait because, so long as I kept my distance, she wasn't actually chewing on the packet. For now, at least, she was safe.

Every time she looked a bit bored and moved away from the needles, I told her what a good girl she was. And eventually I got someone to bring me some chicken. Every time she moved away now, I combined the praise with a bit of chicken, although not if the needles were in her mouth, because she might have thought, 'Hang on a minute – if I steal needles, I get a delicious chicken reward. I'll nick that medical kit more often.' In the end, I threw a bit of chicken slightly further away; she went to get it; I moved forward slowly and she looked at me as if to say, 'Whatever, you can have it.'

There are a couple of morals to that story. First, you're never going to beat a dog for speed, so if you make a grab for something, chances are they'll beat you to it and swallow whatever it is they're guarding. I know it might sound counter-intuitive, but you're far better off taking your time and thinking about a plan of action. Second, chicken tastes better than needles.

Do dogs dream?

You may have seen your dog growling, barking and howling while asleep, while flailing his legs around, and concluded that he's chasing squirrels in a dream. But while it's become widely accepted that dogs dream, we can't know for sure – although some of the finest doggy scientists are on the case. (That's human scientists who study dogs, of course. Doggy scientists aren't on the case at all. They already know.)

Research has also shown that dogs, like humans, go through cycles of non-Rapid Eye Movement (REM) sleep and REM sleep. Humans dream most vividly during REM sleep, and it's inferred from the fact that dogs' eyes dart from side to side beneath their eyelids while they're in REM, as well as the shallow breathing and twitching, that the same thing is happening with them.

A couple of American studies have suggested that rats dream. One of the studies involved rats running around a circular track for a food reward, then compared the rats' subsequent REM-sleep episodes, and extrapolated that the rats were recalling the experience of running around the track while asleep. Similar experiments have been done on cats and mice, so the same is probably going on with dogs.

In humans, part of the brain called the pons is responsible for paralysing the large muscles during sleep, which is what stops people acting out their dreams. Dogs also have a pons, and when the pons is switched off temporarily during studies, dogs start doing doggy activities in their sleep, like chasing things.

If dogs do dream, they're unlikely to be having the surreal dreams humans do; they're more likely to be recollecting mundane stuff that happened that day. Until we can speak to them, we may never know, but I do like to think mine are dreaming while they're curled up in their beds, because the thought of them having fun in their sleep is just cute.

Do dogs like travel?

One of the main reasons people get dogs is to go on all sorts of adventures with them: long walks in the country, trips to the seaside, city breaks. Pretty much everything you want to do when you meet a new partner!

But those dreams can turn to dust if your dog's not a fan of travelling, whether that's riding in a car or taking a train. Never mind weekends away, even popping to the shops can be really hard work if you're having to spend half an hour getting your dog into the back seat of your car.

Some dogs never have problems with cars. And they soon learn to associate them with fun trips to the park, the beach, the lake, or wherever. But it's easy to understand why some dogs don't like them. People know what cars are and they're completely normal to us, but to an animal, something moving underneath them can feel like an earthquake. Everything about the experience screams *Wrong! Wrong! Wrong!* Puppies often get motion sickness, for the same reason young children do – the structures in their inner ear used for balance aren't fully developed yet – and some never grow out of it.

It's best to get your puppy used to travelling as soon as possible, although even dogs who have been travelling in cars since they were puppies can suddenly turn against it. Maybe their last trip in the car was to the vets, where they had a stressful experience. Now every time you lead them to the car, they tremble and lick their lips, with their tail tucked between their legs.

If you've got a dog who hates being in the car, you need to employ something called reassociation training, otherwise known as counterconditioning, which is when you take a situation that has negative associations and turn it into a situation with positive associations. In other words, you need to teach your dog that when she gets into the car, good things will happen, and she's not necessarily going to end up at the vets.

My first piece of advice is to act as normally as possible, as if getting into the car is the most natural thing in the world. If you're hesitant, your dog will be hesitant as well. And instead of doing what you see lots of people doing, namely trying to shove their dog in from behind (which will leave your dog thinking, 'Why? I don't see you getting in!'), lead by example: without going anywhere, try getting in the car first and encouraging your dog to join you, perhaps for a tasty treat. There's nothing like a bit of FOMO (fear of missing out) for this. If your dog's thinking, 'That looks like a good place to be. I wanna be there too!' you've made a great start.

Going for a drive is all about breaking things down into small steps:

Step one: If your dog is motivated by food, maybe give him a little breakfast or dinner in the car instead of in the house.

Step two: Having done this for a few days without attempting to take the dog for a ride, get in the front seat and close the doors with him inside.

Step three: This time, switch the engine on, but don't go anywhere.

Step four: Nudge the car forwards and back on your front drive.

Step five: Go for a drive around the block.

If it sounds painstaking, it is. But if you go too fast, you'll end up back at square one. You won't get through all of these steps in a day if you're doing it right, but two weeks of training will be time well spent if your precious pooch travels happily ever after.

Think about your actual driving. Accelerate and brake slower, don't take corners too quickly. It's all about giving your dog as smooth a ride as possible. I also recommend dog-appeasing pheromone (DAP), which is essentially the smell of Mum when she was nursing. Spray it on a dog's bed or blanket, but remember to leave it 20 minutes or so before the dog climbs in, because the carrier for DAP is ethanol, and if your dog gets a whiff of that, shooting up their sensitive nose like smelling salts, it will probably have a less than calming effect.

Then there are dogs who bark all the way to wherever it is you're going, in which case they might just be excited to get there. If you have a dog who barks in the car, think about taking him on some longer journeys. That might sound like hell, but people have reported that once they reach the relative smoothness of a motorway, their dogs calm down. At that point you need to praise him, especially if he lies down, which is a sure sign his anxiety is easing.

You might not be aware that it's against the law in the UK and other countries to have a dog unrestrained in the car, but you can use a crate or attach him to the seat belt (via a harness rather than a collar, in case the worst happens). And it's probably best not to have your dog on the front seat, even if they're small, because however well behaved they usually are, something might spook them, you'll get distracted, and, well … I don't need to tell you how that ends.

As for dogs sticking their heads out of car windows, I know it looks cute and gives passersby a chuckle, but dogs can get dust and debris in their eyes and they have been known to clip tree branches and cyclists. At the risk of sounding like a party pooper, please don't.

If you're planning a long journey, you need to be stopping every couple of hours, so that your dog can stretch his legs, go to the toilet and have some water. And keep them on a lead! I often see people wandering around a service station car park with their dog unleashed, but why would you risk it when you're next to a motorway? It does not make sense to me. Oh, and never leave your dog in a parked car on a warm day, and not just when it's 30 degrees. I read an article a couple of years ago that said that even if it's only 20 degrees outside, within a few minutes of winding up the windows and closing the doors, the temperature inside a car may be warm enough to kill your dog.

In terms of public transport, there's no substitute for getting your puppy on a bus or the Tube as early as you can, because those kinds of trips involve all sorts of sensory experiences that you don't get in a car.

Think about all the strange noises you hear on the Tube: beeping, whooshing, ear-splitting whistling. Add crowds of strangers into the mix and it can be terrifying for a puppy (although at least people say hello on the Tube if you've got a dog!). As with anywhere else, act normal and calm. And I'd also make sure your dog is trained to sit and lie down on command, in lots of different places. Just because your dog responds to commands in your living room, that doesn't necessarily mean he's going to do it on a crowded bus. And you don't want him running for the doors every time they open!

Do dogs grieve?

There has been quite a bit of research into whether dogs grieve, and the outcomes suggest that they do. A 2016 study, carried out by Australian and New Zealand researchers, looked into behavioural changes in dogs that had recently lost a household companion. Those changes included increased affection towards their owner (although some reported less), more sleeping and seeking out their deceased mate's favourite spots, such as where they used to sleep.

I'm convinced dogs do grieve because I've heard so much anecdotal evidence over the years, literally hundreds of cases of owners saying, 'We lost our other dog and he's been flat for ages.' In some cases, the dog had lost a human member of the family and hadn't been the same since.

There is the argument that 'grieving' dogs are just mirroring their owner's behaviour, because they're likely to be grieving too. And some scientists believe it's simply a form of separation anxiety, which makes some sense. Let's say there are two dogs in the house and one of them goes off to the vet one day and never comes back. The surviving dog spends weeks looking out of the window and sniffing the front door. Any time someone enters the house, they look beyond them, wondering if their pal has been brought back. I find those kinds of stories particularly touching.

Whether a dog is grieving or simply suffering from separation anxiety, it often takes them weeks and months to get over it, and I suspect it's a different experience for every dog, as it is with humans.

When a dog loses their human companion, they often get rehomed, as was the case with the late Queen's corgis, Sandy and Muick. The Duchess of York kindly took them in, and they joined her own pack of Norfolk terriers (she's got five of them!).

Sandy and Muick's worlds had been turned upside down, having lost their main human caregiver, moved house and been integrated with a whole new group of friends. We can only imagine how stressful those three events happening at once is to a dog. And whether you're a dog who came from a palace or a council flat, it must be equally as upsetting.

Dogs sometimes become locked into their grief, because every time they look upset or scared, the humans around them seem upset and scared, too. It can be a downward spiral. The solution is to use positive body language, as best you can, to show the dog that all is well with the world, even if it's not really. There's something very comforting about being with a person who seems to be calm and happy; it rubs off.

It's impossible to predict how long it will take your dog to start feeling themselves again. When I chatted to the duchess on ITV's *This Morning*, she explained it had taken Muick (pronounced 'Mick', in case you were wondering) quite some time to get over the Queen's passing and start being himself again, although I have seen cases where dogs turn around very quickly. Take your time and resist your natural tendency to show quite how sorry you feel for them. Show them that while life might be different, it's still good.

Do dogs get depressed?

Given how similar our brains are to dog brains, it's not that surprising that our canine friends can get depressed, just like us.

In 2022, the charity Guide Dogs published research that suggested 74 per cent of UK dogs (from a poll of a thousand owners) showed signs of poor mental health such as anxiety and depression.

Signs include being withdrawn, lethargy, loss of appetite, restlessness and not keeping to usual sleeping patterns, hiding, chewing, aggression or going to the toilet where they shouldn't. They might also start following owners around more than normal, or lie on their belly a lot and open their eyes as soon as you move, suggesting they're bored and want something to do.

Things that might trigger depression include changes to a dog's environment or routine (maybe you've moved and got a new job with different hours) and changes to their social group (like Stanley, maybe your other dog has died or your kids have upped sticks and gone off to university). It's also been suggested that dogs get a form of Seasonal Affective Disorder (SAD) in the darker, colder months, but it might just be that your dogs aren't getting as much exercise, because a dog walk when it's cold, dark and muddy is a far less attractive proposition than a dog walk when it's warm and sunny.

The research by the aforementioned Dr Berns at Emory University also suggests that dogs get depressed, and I've met plenty who seemed that way, often ones who were stuck home alone all day. Some would be going stir crazy and climbing the walls (literally), usually collies and German shepherds, which were bred to work and need physical and mental stimulation. But other dogs would just seem a bit fed up. I'd observe their body language and think, 'Yep, he's just like a depressed human who's lacking in energy and can't get out of bed.'

The deeper a dog falls into a funk, the scarier the outside world will seem. Just getting out the front door will feel like climbing Everest. But while you should never tell a person to man up or snap out of it – poor mental health is a lot more complicated in humans – with dogs, things can be a lot easier to deal with. Jolly them along a bit, get them out for a good walk, play around with them in the garden, maybe involving treats as rewards and/or interactive games (google 'canine enrichment') – you'll be surprised at the difference it all can make. Just don't force the issue.

* * *

Who knows what Dr Berns and his ilk will discover with their brain scanners and equipment not yet invented in the coming years? Maybe in 10, 20 or 30 years' time, we'll be fairly certain that dogs feel a lot more than the basic emotions.

Perhaps one day we'll read about an experiment that shows dogs are amused by humans falling over, or get embarrassed by their owners' attempts at dressing them up, or feel pride and contentment at completing certain tasks. And, whisper it quietly, perhaps we'll all understand the concept of love. One day ...

Chapter 2

Can Dogs Read Our Minds?

Scientists have been attempting to answer this question for decades, and we'll probably never know the answer. My hunch is that dogs can't read minds, simply because humans, as intelligent as we are, aren't able to do it (although there have been some very impressive stage acts that came close).

But if we forget about mind-reading and think of it more in terms of *Do dogs sometimes know what we're thinking?* there's lots of evidence that suggests they do.

For a long time, people believed that a dog 'understanding' a human was actually a combination of learnt behaviour and owners projecting human traits onto their dog. But that was before the science of canine cognition took off in the 1990s. Nowadays, it's difficult to read a newspaper without coming across some new study about how dogs do or don't understand their owners.

Studies have shown that dogs can pick up on emotional cues in speech. They've shown that dogs can be influenced by a human's social cues (in 2012, University of Milan researchers showed that humans could convince dogs to opt for a smaller portion of food by reacting more positively towards it than the bigger portion – if only that worked on me!). They've shown that dogs can interpret subtle changes in a human's tone of voice and gaze. They've shown that dogs are able to *recognise* and *understand* human emotions, which goes beyond merely being able to differentiate between them.

Not that I'm trying to downplay the cleverness of all these scientists, but it's not that surprising that dogs understand us so well. Humans have probably been selecting dogs specifically for their smartness for hundreds of generations – and when your survival depends on someone else, as a dog's does with us, it's probably best that you've got at least some idea what they're thinking.

Can dogs 'catch' our emotions?

There is lots of evidence for human-like personality traits in dogs, including four of the so-called 'big five':

1. Openness to experience (inventive/curious v. consistent/cautious)
2. Extraversion (outgoing/energetic v. solitary/reserved)
3. Agreeableness (friendly/compassionate v. critical/rational)
4. Neuroticism (sensitive/nervous v. resilient/confident)
5. Conscientiousness (efficient/organised v. extravagant/careless). This is the only one that doesn't appear to exist in dogs.

Where humans and dogs are most similar seems to be in the realms of extraversion and neuroticism. Evidence suggests that an outgoing, energetic owner is more likely to have an outgoing, energetic dog, while a sensitive, nervous owner is more likely to have a sensitive, nervous dog.

Scientists believe those similarities develop over time, and one theory is that it's a survival mechanism: it's easier for two individuals, whether they be humans or dogs, to negotiate life, and all its challenges, if they're on the same wavelength.

We live in a world where it's OK not to be OK, so people are far more honest about their mental health than they used to be. But that sometimes leads to owners projecting their mental health issues onto their dogs.

I once met an Australian cattle dog whose owners were convinced he was anxious. He was pulling like crazy to get out of the front door, he was biting his lead, he was biting the grass in front of him. One of the first things I said to the owners was, 'How do you feel?' They replied, 'We're really anxious.' I knew that was what they were going to say!

This dog wasn't anxious at all, he was just very excited – desperate – to go and do the job he was bred for: 'Come on! Let's go and find some cattle!'

However, had those owners continued to assume their dog was anxious, there was a chance he might have become so, because anxiety tends to be contagious.

Several recent studies, including one in 2021 by the Canine Science Collaboratory at Arizona State University, have shown that dogs can 'catch' emotions from their owners, through behavioural and chemical cues (changing of the owner's body odour and the release of various hormones, including oxytocin). Scientists call this 'interspecies emotional contagion'.

So if an owner is calm and confident, their dog tends to feel safe and secure. And if an owner is stressed and anxious, their dog can feel stressed and anxious as well. Funny, that. The research also shows that a dog who spends a lot of time with their owner is more likely to 'catch' their owner's emotions than a dog who hangs out less often with their human, maybe having an owner who works five days a week for a few hours a day.

Sometimes, I can work out a dog's breed just by speaking to their owner, which might be contagion, but is just as likely to be evidence that certain types of people feel natural affinity with certain types of dogs.

In my early days working with dogs, I'd listen to an owner on the phone – how fast they spoke, how calm or agitated they sounded – then listen to the description of their dog's behavioural problem. And if they hadn't already told me, I'd try to guess what breed it was.

True story: one day, a lady phoned me, and she was speaking very quickly and sounded highly agitated. I'd almost describe her as hyperactive, because I couldn't get a word in edgeways. Sure enough, she explained that her dog was also hyperactive, and would almost pull her through the front door when he wanted to go for a walk. The fact she was also clearly a very intelligent person convinced me that she owned either a German shepherd or a Border collie, although I couldn't work out which (in case you were wondering, German shepherds and Border collies would both be in the top set at dog school).

When I was finally able to speak, and asked what breed of dog it was, she said, 'Oh, she's a Border collie crossed with a

German shepherd? I can't tell you how pleased I was with myself. Simple things please simple minds and all that . . .

When I got to this lady's house, her dog was demonstrating obsessive behaviours, such as chasing shadows and reflections dancing on the wall. Most Labradors won't be at all bothered by a shadow or the reflection of a watch, but it's not at all uncommon for collies. Then again, it wouldn't do for us all to be the same. Or our dogs.

Do dogs judge people?

A 2023 Austrian study suggested that dogs judge humans to some extent and are more patient with people who are incompetent than people who are cruel.

In this study, researchers took 96 dogs and put each one behind a clear screen, with a researcher on the other side. In this screen were holes, just big enough to pass food through. The researchers then behaved in two distinct ways. The first group – 'the meanies' – showed the dogs a treat but quickly pulled it back again just before it reached a hole. I don't think they were flicking the dogs V signs, but they were certainly teasing them. The second group (I'll call them 'the incompetents') 'accidentally' dropped the food – whoops-a-daisy! – just before it reached the hole.

The two groups of dogs tended to behave differently towards the researchers depending on whether they were being 'mean' or 'incompetent'. They'd ignore the researchers who had teased them, breaking off eye contact and wandering away, just as you'd do if someone was teasing you. But with the second group of researchers, the dogs tended to hang around with their noses poking through the hole, perhaps thinking, 'Go on, mate! Try again! I know you can do it!' Apparently, they believed the researchers wanted to feed them but were too clumsy to do so. Isn't that sweet?

This suggests dogs may have *theory of mind* – the ability to attribute thoughts to others and infer their behaviours – which puts them in an exclusive club that includes chimpanzees, horses and humans from one year old.

A lot of dog studies involve simply watching and inferring, and what's interesting is that the science often confirms what most experienced dog owners thought anyway, because those kinds of experiments happen naturally in people's homes every day.

If you said to ten owners, 'Do you think your dog knows when you've stood on their paw by accident – as opposed to being a horrible cruel person who meant it – I think most of them would say yes. They'd have been cooking one day, with their pooch lurking behind them, hoping for a tasty morsel, and they'd have stepped backwards and heard a yelp. (Guilty!) But as long as you give them a little stroke and say sorry, your dog won't hold it against you, because they'll know you've just been a well-meaning clumsy galoot. Humans and dogs have been interacting long enough for them to understand when they're being mistreated deliberately or not. If you're reading this book, you're almost by definition a dog lover: it's reassuring they know that although we might be incompetent buffoons sometimes, we're never meanies, right?

Does my dog know when I'm angry?

Some scientists, and indeed philosophers, are still of the belief that dogs don't have theory of mind, and instead react to stimuli in the environment without conscious thought. The jury is out. But there's no doubt that dogs are brilliant at reading facial expressions and subtle clues in body language, just like humans.

For a long time, it was assumed that dogs focused more on human body language – hunched shoulders, moping, that kind of stuff – than facial cues. But a 2018 Italian study suggested that dogs respond to human facial expressions of six basic emotions – anger, fear, happiness, sadness, surprise and disgust – with changes in gaze and heart rate. That's not too surprising given that humans and dogs evolved together over tens of thousands of years.

One British study found that dogs engaged in mouth-licking when people looked at them angrily, but not when they heard angry human voices, which suggests the dogs were reacting to visual clues. (While we're on the subject, forget what people say about not smiling at dogs, 'because showing teeth is aggressive in their world' – they can absolutely differentiate between smiling and snarling.)

Mouth-licking is an 'appeasement behaviour', which serves to prevent or reduce aggressive behaviour, usually in a dog buddy. However, dogs were more likely to mouth-lick when looking at images of angry humans than of other dogs, which suggests dogs got wiser to human facial expressions to get on better with us.

Dogs can often react quite badly when humans argue. One of our Rottweilers, sadly no longer with us, would start barking and getting quite uppity if people were having a barney (usually at the wrong person, in my opinion, ahem ...), but other dogs will shy away. An uppity Rottie turns out to be a pretty good deterrent to bickering, incidentally. If something like this happens to you, you may find that even after you've gone out, returned with a nice bottle of something and are cuddling on the sofa, he'll still be looking at you as if to say, 'Is everything OK here?' They're not daft.

Does my dog know when I'm happy or sad?

It's becoming a theme of this book that the science just proves what most dog owners already knew, or at least suspected. You're always hearing people saying things like, 'My dog knows when I'm under the weather or a bit down; they come and give me a cuddle.' Your dog won't know the ins and outs of why you're a bit flat and/or teary – that you've had a row with your best human friend, missed out on a promotion or you're feeling a bit rough because you're not sleeping properly – but they know something's going on. And sharing each other's feelings brings you and your dog even closer together. It really is a lovely thing. Does your dog love you? I, for one, would forgive you for thinking so!

You may be reading this and thinking, 'But isn't this just confirmation bias? We see what we want to see. We think our dogs are cuddling us because they know we're suffering in some way, but they probably would have cuddled us anyway.'

I'm sure there's an element of that going on. Let's say you're normally a busy, bustling person and you don't spend much time lounging on the sofa. You might not cuddle your dog much, but that doesn't mean your dog doesn't want to. Then one day, you'll walk through the door and flop straight down on the sofa because you're feeling a bit rubbish, the dog will jump onto your lap and you'll be thinking, 'How wonderful, he's cuddling me because he knows how I'm feeling.' Not quite. He's being a cuddly opportunist, which isn't quite the same!

We do have to be aware of confirmation bias when it comes to dogs, because humans are good at kidding themselves, but I'm also convinced that dogs know roughly what we're feeling and act accordingly. And at the risk of getting overly philosophical, if it makes us feel good, does it really matter if we're kidding ourselves?

In any case, as I mentioned earlier, the science backs up most owners' instincts: a 2017 University of Naples study suggested that dogs can smell whether we're happy (and that they become happier as a result if we are), while a 2022 University of Belfast study suggested that dogs can sniff out stress in their owners. Dogs have also been proven to have 'affective empathy', which is the ability to understand someone else's feelings and respond appropriately.

So, if dogs can 'read' your emotions to some degree, do those feelings affect your dog's own emotions? Generally speaking, a happy owner will have a happy dog – and an unhappy dog almost always makes for an unhappy owner! I see that every day, and as a dog trainer it's my job to try to up the happiness quotient for both parties when the relationship goes wrong.

However, not all dogs are made anxious by anxious owners, and some dogs can be trained to sense anxiety attacks and provide comfort and support, such as licking their owner's hand or laying their head on their lap.

Research has shown that when owners and their dogs interact, or even just look into each other's eyes, oxytocin is released in both owner and dog in a feedback loop. As we've already seen, oxytocin goes by the nickname the 'love hormone' or 'cuddle hormone', but what oxytocin actually does is facilitate attention, which enables dogs to recognise the emotions of their owner.

As for whether humans can 'catch' emotions from dogs, that's an area that hasn't been looked into much, at least not in scientific settings. But most owners of nervous and anxious dogs will tell you that their dogs make them nervous and anxious at times, so it's probably true that a happy dog – one that comes bounding towards you with his tail wagging before licking your face (or trying to!) – will also make his owner happier. And science can tell us how good humans are at reading positive and negative emotion from dogs' facial expressions (although it can't tell us *exactly* what the emotions are).

Can dogs sense fear?

Evidence suggests that dogs are better at reading their owners than the average person on the street. That's no real surprise, given the amount of time a dog and his owner spend with each other. And one thing dogs are particularly good at is picking up on human fear.

Until recently, it was just a theory that dogs could smell fear. You'd hear it all the time: 'Don't be scared around a dog: they will smell it and attack you.' But scientists from the University of Naples seem to have proved the theory to be true.

They found that when dogs were exposed to body odour from strangers in a happy state, they were more likely to interact and had lower heart rates. But dogs who were exposed to odour from fearful strangers displayed more stress behaviours, had higher heart rates (suggesting they were fearful themselves) and sought more reassurance from their owners. The specific smell the dogs were reacting less favourably to was probably adrenaline, which humans can't pick up on.

However – and it's a big however – it can't always be the smell of fear that dogs pick up on, because you often see a dog barking and lunging at someone on the other side of the street, and it's not credible that the person's adrenaline can waft that far in an instant. Instead, that barking, lunging dog is probably reacting to visual clues, such as a human's widening eyes, sideways looks, the tensing of the body.

Often when a dog reacts to a scared person, it's because they're scared themselves. It's similar with humans: if you're down the pub and someone is lurking in the corner, looking on edge and unpredictable, you might think, 'What the hell is this bloke going to do next?' And you might want the landlord to sling them out before something goes off.

For a dog, making that scared person squirm, recoil or look away by barking and lunging at them will make them feel better: 'Ha! Excellent, got rid of them.' However, some dogs – especially guard dogs and specially trained attack dogs – won't be scared at all; they just get a kick out of terrifying people, because that's what they were bred and taught (rewarded) to do.

Whatever the motivation, it's not great for humans who are nervous of dogs, because it creates a vicious circle (pardon the pun): their fear brings out the worst in dogs, so they become even more fearful, validating why they didn't like dogs in the first place.

Can dogs spot a liar?

A series of studies by Kyoto University suggest that dogs will only use information and follow commands from people they've decided are trustworthy. Isn't that interesting?

In one experiment, researchers presented the dogs with two containers, one with treats and toys hidden inside and one that was empty. In the first round, a researcher pointed to the container with toys and treats so the dogs knew where to find the goodies. In round two, they pointed to the container that was empty, deliberately tricking the dogs so they went to the wrong location. In round three, they pointed to the container that was filled with treats once more. But this time, some of the dogs no longer trusted the researcher – although, intriguingly, they did trust a new researcher in round four. This experiment suggests that dogs judge the reliability of humans based on their lies and are even more sophisticated in terms of social intelligence than we thought. You might say – and I have for years – that you can fool a dog, but you might only fool him once . . .

Another Kyoto experiment was designed to find out whether dogs can tell if a person is being rude to another person or not, and if that information affects their opinion of the person. In the experiment, a dog watched their owner struggle to open a container, before asking a stranger for help. Sometimes the stranger helped, sometimes they refused. After each struggle session, the dog was given the choice to accept attention from the stranger or ignore them. And, you've guessed it, when the stranger refused to help the dog's owner, the dog was more likely to ignore them. This ties in with so many stories I've heard from people along the lines of, 'I knew my dog was on to something when he steered clear of my new boyfriend! What a bad man he turned out to be . . .'

Chapter 3

Relationship Counselling for Dogs and People

We know that dogs learn by copying other dogs, which is called social learning.

In short, social learning is when youngsters, of whatever species, observe the behaviour of older individuals and learn which behaviours are likely to be beneficial to them or not. But domestic dogs don't grow up in the wild, as part of a pack; they grow up in houses surrounded by humans. Which begs the question: do domestic dogs copy human behaviour in the same way as wild dogs copy the behaviour of their mums and packmates?

A 2018 Hungarian study set out to answer this question by asking a group of eight-week-old puppies to solve a couple of puzzles. The details of the puzzles aren't that important (they involved opening boxes with bits of sausage inside), but the results were. The puppies were *slightly* more likely to solve the puzzles after watching their mum do it first (5 per cent), which wasn't a surprise, but they were *far* more likely to solve the puzzle after watching an unfamiliar dog do it first (29 per cent). Why? Well, the researchers speculated that the puppies were more likely to closely observe a strange dog's behaviour than their mum's.

The researchers then ran the experiment using people to open the boxes instead of dogs. Remarkably, the puppies were now 42 per cent more likely to solve the puzzles, meaning they learnt more from watching a human's behaviour than the behaviour of another dog. In conclusion, the lead researcher said, 'We can train puppies from a young age by showing them what to do, like their mothers. If we want them to fetch a stick, we should fetch it first, and if a person wants them to use a new bed, they should lie down in it first.'

However – and this is an important distinction – the puppies weren't *copying* the humans or the adult dogs, because while some adult dogs used their snouts to open the boxes and others used their paws, and obviously all the humans used their hands, all the puppies used their snouts. That suggests their brains were working at a deeper level – they were deciphering how the boxes worked before using their own method to open them.

If only training a dog was as easy as showing them what to do a couple of times and then watching them do it (although if that were the case, I'd probably still be in advertising!). It reminds me of a cartoon strip I once saw of a man trying to toilet train his dog to cock a leg on a tree: after a few failed attempts, in the last sequence, exasperated, he's having a wee himself against the tree, pointing and saying, 'Look!' It's a funny image, but in reality, I think we all know that's not going to work.

Instead, we have to be a lot cuter when training dogs – and a lot more patient! Sitting there quietly is not going to convince a dog who's barking at the neighbour's dog to be quiet, but if you combine quietness with other elements – and are prepared to put the time in – you might yet solve the problem.

It's all about understanding that while domestic dogs were once wild, they've now been hanging about with humans for thousands of years. We've co-evolved, so our environment is their environment, which informs so many, if not all, of our interactions, whether we know it or not.

Should I tell my dog off?

Have you ever worked for a boss who should never have been promoted because they're actually not very good at that higher level? Maybe they're now a manager, despite the fact they're not great with people and get stressed out easily. People still like them outside of work, but in an office environment they've become a bit of a nightmare. Well, I met a dog like that recently.

When I say I met him, I actually saw him on a video. This little dog was barking like mad every time someone walked past the door. If someone knocked on the door, he turned into that girl from *The Exorcist*. And I thought, 'I know what's going on here, this dog's been overpromoted and got too big for his boots. His owner needs to step up and show a bit of leadership.'

Leadership is a tricky one when it comes to dog training, because it's – wrongly – become synonymous with domination, even bullying, and has understandably gone slightly out of fash-ion. But proper leadership has got nothing to do with domination and bullying, or 'showing who's boss'. Instead it's about helping people – and dogs – understand what their roles are and letting them get on with it. Leading by example, creating conditions for others to willingly follow: *that's* what leadership is about for me, with the emphasis on 'willingly'. What's wrong with that?

It was clear that this dog's owner had given him the job of defending the house, even though he wasn't very good at it. I'm sure she'd never sat the dog down and told him this, but he's got to thinking, 'It looks like one of us has got to repel all these invaders,' which is why he looked like he wanted to rip someone's head off every time the postman put a letter through the box. He wasn't a nasty dog but – under pressure, in a role he wasn't suited to – he was trying too hard.

What the owner needed to do was try to see things from the dog's point of view. If that dog could explain himself, he'd probably say, 'Every time I bark, the invaders go away.' To which the owner would reply, 'No, you've misunderstood. They're not going away because you're barking, they're just on their way to the shop at the end of the road or off to deliver some more letters.' The dog might say, 'Nah. I barked, they ran away. What part of that don't you understand?' and it would be the owner's job to convince them otherwise: 'Mate, don't worry about it. You don't have to be the supervisor any more, it doesn't suit you. Just chill out, I'll deal with the invaders.' Of course, owners need to do this in language dogs understand, which is the language of rewarding the right moments and staying calm, even when things are getting stressful. Good leaders never panic. Or at least, they don't appear to, which ultimately, is good enough.

Dominant leadership is less accepted in society nowadays across the board. Rightly so. Whether you're the manager of a football team or the manager in an office, you're expected to have softer skills and not just bark out orders.

While I would never endorse any methods that were cruel and caused physical or emotional pain, I do think that we've got a bit confused when it comes to leadership and our dogs. I've even heard dog trainers say to people, 'You must never say no to your dog', even though we know that if we never say no to our children, things can turn out ugly (just read *Charlie and the Chocolate Factory*!).

Recently, I met a dog who had taken over his owner's house. We took him out for a quick walk, and it soon became clear what was going on. We'd gone no more than ten feet from the front door when he stopped to sniff and wee on a lamppost. He'd stop every time he saw one – or a tree, or a bin, or a bollard, or anything that was sticking out of the ground – and it took us about ten minutes to reach the end of the street. It's quite a familiar routine for many dog owners.

The owners had read that they should let their dog 'explore the world', so if he wanted to stop for a sniff and a wee, they'd let him. In fact, they let him do whatever he wanted to do, whenever, inside and outside the house. But if you were out walking with your child and they kept stopping every few yards, before saying, 'OK, you may now proceed', you'd say to them, 'Come on, mate, we've got to go.' If they persisted, you'd eventually tell them to behave themselves, because we accept that parents should have some level of control over their children and be allowed to correct them if they're not doing what they're told. It's about finding the right balance.

When it comes to dogs, we seem to have got ourselves into a place where we think we're never allowed to correct them and that everything we say to them has to be positive. Don't misunderstand me here: positive is good and you'll get nowhere without rewarding the good behaviours, but correcting your dog doesn't mean bellowing at or beating them, just as it doesn't mean bellowing at or beating your child.

There are other things you can do: use your facial expressions (the 'I'm so disappointed in you' look), change your tone of voice, or simply say, 'Oi, no!' (don't worry, the dog won't understand that 'oi' is rude in human-speak; it's just a noise to them).

In a similar vein, I met a very nice lady who'd been living on her own for ten years with her lovely black Labrador, who was also a female. This black Lab had become very reactive to all sorts of movements and sounds and wouldn't let anybody apart from her owner into the house. If her owner phoned anybody, she'd bark the house down. If her owner took her anywhere, she'd make a right old racket. So in the end, her owner stopped taking her to places.

The owner described her dog's behaviour as 'controlling', which I thought was really interesting. I sat her down and said, 'If you had a boyfriend who didn't allow anyone else in the house, who didn't like you phoning anyone, who shouted and screamed because he didn't like the company you were keeping, you wouldn't put up with it, because that's the very definition of a controlling boyfriend. You might even say a narcissist. So, when are you going to tell your dog to stop doing the same?' The good news is, it's easier to stop your dog from being controlling than it is to stop a coercive partner.

My three and a half golden rules are as follows:

1. Any behaviour that feels rewarding will increase (which is why praise and treats work so well).

2. Any behaviour that feels uncomfortable will decrease (by uncomfortable, I don't mean screaming at or hitting your dog – that dirty look can sometimes do the job).

3. Some behaviours that are ignored will fade away (although the tricky part is knowing which behaviours to ignore – attention seeking, usually).

3½. Practice doesn't always make perfect – practise the wrong way, and you could make things worse (this is more of an observation than a rule, hence it doesn't get its own number).

If these rules sound manipulative, well, yeah, dog training is all about manipulation in a sense, but for a good reason. Somebody has to take the lead, whether it's you or your dog, so it might as well be you. If you don't, your dog may move into the vacuum and start manipulating you instead, whether that means assuming the role of supervisor and yapping at the door all day or getting so upset about their owner making phone calls and meeting people that she hardly ever speaks to anyone.

So, in short: it is OK to tell your dog off, but just be mindful of how you do it. For more information on the golden rules and how to use them, see my book, *All Dogs Great and Small*.

Does my dog like affection?

A few years back, the famous dog expert Stanley Coren caused a bit of an uproar in the dog world by suggesting that some dogs don't like being hugged.

Professor Coren's theory was that because dogs are 'cursorial' animals, in other words designed to run, their first line of defence is to leg it. As such, 'depriving a dog of that course of action by immobilising him with a hug can increase his stress level'.

To prove his point, Coren looked at 250 randomly sourced pictures of people hugging dogs and concluded that 81.6 per cent of them showed dogs who were exhibiting at least one sign of discomfort, stress or anxiety (including turning their heads away, showing 'half-moon eyes', which is when the whites of a dog's eyes become more prominent, lowered ears, lip-licking, yawning and raising a paw) and only 7.6 per cent of them showed dogs who were comfortable.

Professor Coren's suggestions were controversial for a couple of reasons. First, they were made in an internet column and were, by his own admission, casual observations, not part an official, peer-reviewed study. Second, and probably more significantly, most people are convinced that their dogs adore being hugged!

However, several dog behaviourists were quoted in the media as saying that while Professor Coren's findings can't be taken at face value, and that more research is needed, they too advised against hugging dogs, with one pointing out that hugging is a primate behaviour and not something dogs do naturally (which isn't really surprising, because they don't have arms!).

What's certain is that some dogs like human contact more than others, and it depends on whether we're talking about full-on cuddles (which some dogs will find restrictive) or a loose embrace. And it's always best to tell children not to hug strange dogs, because they might get bitten.

It's possible to pass our negative feelings on to a dog through touch. I was once sitting in a pub with a lady and her dog who kept barking at anyone who walked past. And every time this happened, the lady picked her dog up and stroked her. But it was clear that while she thought the stroking might calm her dog, she was also doing it to calm herself. As a result, the dog started thinking, 'When you stroke me like that, you must be nervous. And if you're nervous, I need to defend you.'

Personally, I think it's another case of horses for courses. I'm all for cuddling dogs; I do it with mine all the time. But if you've got a dog who wriggles out of attempted hugs, there are lots of other ways to show affection, such as good old-fashioned stroking and sitting with your arm around him on the sofa. And what self-respecting dog doesn't like a tummy tickle from the right person, eh?

One thing most dogs love is being scratched. Sometimes when you scratch a dog behind the ears or at the bottom of his spine, he'll narrow his eyes, widen his mouth and break into what looks like a satisfied smile. It might sound weird that scratching what might otherwise be called the 'bum area' (the base of the tail) could be a superior alternative to head stroking, but a lot of dogs are head-shy.

We all need a bit of affection, whether we admit it or not, but maybe just think about the timing when doling it out to your dog. If he's been a good boy and he jumps on your lap, stroke away. If he's being naughty right now, think twice.

Having a companion who loves you unconditionally is one of the biggest reasons for people getting a dog, but sometimes your dog can become more of a shadow than a companion, and more of a pest than a pet.

I recently moved house with my partner and our three dogs. It took a little while for all of them to settle down, but it was especially challenging for our 16-year-old Patterdale terrier, Tish, who is now almost completely blind.

The other two dogs, who are also getting on a bit, seemed to twig pretty quickly that it was a new place, understood where their bed was, and went back to a normal sleeping pattern. But Tish really struggled. She'd go in the garden to do her business and we'd have to bring her back in again because she couldn't find the door. She'd then follow us around, almost obsessively. I think it gave her great comfort to know that there was some-body's leg a couple of feet away. Even if we sat down at the kitchen island, she'd constantly tap around, never really settling.

Tish's behaviour was to be expected, but for her benefit and our sanity it was important to make her understand that every-thing was fine. So every time she started to get restless, or follow us around, or obsessively walk in circles, I'd pick her up, put her in her bed, soothe her and wait to see what happened next. If she got out and walked around again, I'd gently pick her up and do the same. But if she put her head down like the other two, I'd praise her, give her a soothing stroke and stay with her until she fell asleep. By doing that, I was teaching her that it's okay to settle. We've been in the house for three months now and only in the last month has she started to settle regularly. It's a work in progress.

At the other end of the spectrum, some owners just have to accept that their dogs aren't as friendly as they'd like them to be.

For example, while lots of people will tell you how cuddly their French bulldog is (French bulldogs are essentially minia-turised English bulldogs that were taken to France by Nottingham lacemakers in the 19th century, before ending up as companion dogs for society ladies), the fact is some French bulldogs are quite aloof. When their owner wants them to be snuggled up beside them on the sofa, they'll be curled up in their basket, star-ing at their owner as if to say, 'I wasn't really bred to be a pet, I was bred to bait bulls.'

Even breeds that have been lap dogs for hundreds of years have their outliers. Maybe you've got a bichon frise, which were companion dogs at royal courts as long ago as the 13th century and are normally quite needy, and his general attitude is, 'Stop bothering me. I don't want to be close to you, just let me kip over here in peace.'

Often an owner who craves cuddles will try to cajole their dog into submission: 'Come to Daddy, come to Daddy. Love me, love me, love me. PLEASE LOVE ME!' But you can't force a naturally solitary, independent dog to show you affection. They love you in their own way, and they're cool with being around you, but they're not that bothered about cuddles.

Again, there are similarities with human-on-human relation-ships. Imagine someone has their eye on you as a potential romantic partner and are quite full-on. Maybe they're bom-barding you with texts, and if you don't reply within half an hour, because you're busy at work, they get agitated: 'Is every-thing OK? Are you all right? Are we all right? Do you still like me?' After a few weeks of this, you might start thinking, 'This is a big red flag. I'm going to have to tell them it's off.'

Interestingly, you rarely hear cat people saying, 'Why won't my cat love me?' They just accept that their moggy will do whatever she wants. But some dog people *expect* their dog to dote on them all the time – as if it was part of the terms and conditions when they got them.

It probably doesn't help that there are loads of famous stories about faithful dogs, some of them apocryphal. In Edinburgh, there's a statue of Greyfriars Bobby, who was a Skye or Dandie Dinmont terrier who became famous for spending 14 years guarding his owner's grave before his own death in 1872.

A few years ago, a scientist called Jan Bondeson from the University of Cardiff wrote a book that exploded the myth of Greyfriars Bobby. Bondeson found that graveyard dogs were quite common in the 19th century. They'd make graveyards their home because they'd be fed by visitors, who believed that the dogs were 'guarding' their former owner's resting place. And it seems that an enterprising church warden of Greyfriars Kirkyard, where Bobby's owner was buried, realised he could make a few quid out of this cute terrier.

This guy spread the story that Bobby hadn't left his owner's graveside since he was buried, and the *Scotsman* even published an article about him, which increased visitor numbers and brought money into the community.

Bondeson also speculated that the original Bobby died in 1867 and was replaced by another dog. Bondeson even suggested the local council were in on it (I don't know why he was quite so desperate to debunk the Greyfriars Bobby legend, but apparently he spent untold hours poring over council meeting minutes from the 1860s).

There's also the Japanese story of Hachikō, who would greet his owner at the station every day after his commute home from work. And after Hachikō's owner died, he continued to wait at the station every day, until his own death almost ten years later. Since then, he's been celebrated in Japan as an example of unwavering fidelity.

No wonder the story has been made into films and comic books, because it's just so heartwarming. We can imagine how he felt, watching a train pull in and passengers streaming onto the platform: 'Is that him? No. Maybe that's him?' But at the risk of sounding like an old misery-guts, Hachikō probably only missed his master for a few weeks, after which it just became routine.

Plus, it's documented that after an article about him appeared in one of the country's biggest newspapers, commuters started to recognise him and give him treats. If Hachikō could have spoken, and you asked him why he kept coming back, I suspect he would have said, 'I don't really remember why I started, but I do know that I get food and pats on the head every day. It's just what I do.'

Anyway, the point of all this myth busting is that while we love the idea of a dog who will remain loyal even in death, that's probably not how dogs are. Dogs aren't given a job description when they're born. And, whisper it quietly, some dogs are more like cats. Shocker, I know.

Do dogs like to look good?

The short answer to that question is, 'Of course not!' Dogs aren't humans, so they have no concept of fashion. When you do see a dog with perfectly manicured nails, a low flowing mane and wearing a natty little outfit, that's got nothing to do with the dog and everything to do with his or her owner.

However, while you won't find any wild canines who take regular baths, brush their teeth and clip their nails, let alone don Christmas jumpers, that's not to say dog grooming is a bad thing. Humans have bred into domestic dogs the inability to look after themselves the way nature intended, so it's only right that we should intervene.

Owners are always saying to me, 'My dog won't let me cut his nails,' and there will be a variety of reasons for that, including the dog disliking the clacking sound nail clippers make, or because you cut their nails to the quick as a puppy, or the simple fact that that some dogs simply don't like their paws being touched. (I can still remember the annoyance I felt as a child on Sunday nights when my mum used to bath me and cut my nails, not because it hurt, but because it just seemed like such a rigmarole.)

Dogs who regularly walk on pavements tend to wear their nails down anyway (pavement walking is also good for hardening a dog's pads) – but they will still need trimming fairly regularly. Luckily, professional groomers are very good at that sort of thing. However it's done, in most cases trimming has to take place, otherwise there's a greater chance of ingrown nails and nail trauma.

If you do want to clip your dog's nails yourself, maybe because you feel it would be good for bonding, the first piece of advice is not to force your dog into it. Manhandling – maybe one of you holding her down and the other one doing the business – might work when she's a puppy but probably won't when she's a full-grown adult. Instead, it's far better to make the process purely positive.

To avoid a situation where you're chasing your dog all over the house while waving some nail clippers about, introduce the clippers to your puppy at the same time as you give her a treat, maybe just a piece of kibble, then put them away again. Do that quite frequently, and eventually she'll start thinking, 'I don't know what those things are, but they seem like good news to me.'

Then touch her paws with the clippers and tell her what a good girl she is while smiling and giving her another treat. You don't want to come across as anxious, otherwise your dog will be anxious too. It's about breaking the process down into tiny stages and creating a positive association, until you eventually clip a nail.

While most dogs like being brushed, some do not. Some dogs are simply too impatient, while other dogs will have had a bad experience (maybe you accidentally caught a knot and hurt them when they were a puppy). If you've got a rescue, there's a chance they were abused and don't like being touched.

There are many short-haired breeds that don't need regular brushing, but dogs with longer hair can't do without it, because matted hair can be very painful and even restrict mobility. And if you've got a dog with an undercoat, you should probably get yourself a brush that can really delve into that undercoat and remove dead hair.

Most dogs can learn to like being brushed, and the principles are the same as with nail clipping. If your dog will only tolerate being brushed for 20 seconds before showing signs of anxiety, then only brush her for 20 seconds. But while you're brushing her, make sure you give her plenty of praise, at least until she starts kicking up a fuss. What you mustn't do is start telling her what a good girl she is *after* she's started growling, because the more you do that, the more she'll growl. Hopefully, by building up good experiences instead, she'll eventually be comfortable with being brushed from head to toe in one sitting.

It's very common that dogs won't let people brush their teeth, which begs the question, do we really need to be brushing our dogs' teeth anyway? Well, I'm not a qualified vet, but most vets will say you should be doing it, because dogs can get tooth decay and gum disease, just like humans. And a dog with sore teeth is unlikely to be happy, and might cost you a lot of money to fix.

While wild canine species obviously don't have brushes and toothpaste, they do chomp through lots of crunchy stuff, including bones, which brushes their teeth naturally. Therefore, how often you brush your dog's teeth might depend on what you're feeding them.

I fed my Rotties Axel and Gordon raw chicken carcasses from when they were young (feeding cooked chicken bones is very risky because they can splinter, causing injury), and their teeth stayed nice and clean, while dry food is also quite good for keeping a dog's teeth clean through natural abrasion. Another option is cleaning their teeth with a doggy toothbrush and doggy toothpaste.

When it comes to brushing a dog's teeth, be a bit careful if you've just got a rescue, because diving straight in there might end very badly. Whatever the dog, introduce the toothpaste bit by bit. Don't use the human stuff, because dogs prefer meaty flavours to mint (liver flavour toothpaste, anyone? No, me neither, but dogs seem to approve), and I've never met a dog that's been trained to spit out toothpaste! Put a bit of toothpaste on your finger, maybe before dinner when he's hungry, and get him to lick it off. Eventually, he'll begin to realise that this tasty stuff is coming out of a certain tube, and he'll happily watch you squirt it onto a brush. But don't chase him round the living room with the brush; let him come to you. While he's licking it off the brush, give him lots more praise, and then you can graduate to putting the brush in his mouth, and finally introducing the brushing motion.

I've actually seen an American doggy toothpaste that supposedly whitens teeth, which I can't say I'm a fan of. I know from personal experience that whitening toothpaste can make your teeth sensitive, and there's a chance it will do the same to your dog's teeth. Who knows? They can't really tell us, and anyway, for whose benefit would the whitening be? Hardly the dog's ...

Should my dog sleep in my bed?

This is something people feel very strongly about, one way or the other. My answer is, without a shadow of a doubt ... in most cases it really doesn't matter. At least from a behaviour point of view.

When it comes to dogs and beds/sofas, it's personal choice. Your house, your rules. And if you think about packs of wild dogs, they all snuggle up together, because they are very social animals, as are we.

My two Rottweilers had very dark fur, which was one of the reasons we didn't allow them on our bed, or indeed sofa. In fact, we didn't even let them in the living room, because it had oak flooring, which they would have scratched to bits. When Axel died and Gordon was left on his own, I went a bit soft, put some bedding down next to the sofa and invited him to join us. And when Lily came along, I went even softer: she was a rescue and really loved being next to people, so the rule became, 'If we invite you up, you can come up (with a clear voice cue – "up!" – and a pat of the cushion). But if we don't, you can't.' And that really is the key: it's not so much whether your dog is on the sofa or bed, it's who decides – and it should be you.

I wouldn't be sleeping with a dog on the bed, but that's just me. When we go up to bed, two of our dogs go straight to their own, but the boxer chances his arm with us every now and again. He'll jump up, I'll gently but firmly tell him to get off, and he'll give me a look that says, 'Yeah, yeah, I know', before sloping off. And because we've made nice beds for all three of them on the bedroom floor, they're fine with that.

That's our compromise, and it works nicely for us. But as soon as we open the curtains in the morning, all bets are off and the boxer dives on the bed like Superman. That's because we've allowed him to. Some might say we shouldn't have, because it clouds the issue, but I disagree. It's become our family routine, a happy status quo.

Allowing a dog onto your sofa or bed is unlikely to turn them into some mad, vicious, dominant beast, which some people claim will happen, because there are lots of other factors involved in who takes the lead and sets the rules in a human–dog relationship. Saying that, I have come across cases where the dog has decided the sofa or bed is their domain.

I once met a Great Dane who would push his dad off the marital bed. That was quite comical – they were both big lads, but dad always ended up on the floor – but there was a serious side to it. Then there was the guy with a Jack Russell who'd started dating a lady with two French bulldogs. Because they both allowed their dogs to sleep on their beds when they were on their own, the three dogs would be all over the bed when they were together.

As you can imagine, that wasn't doing much for their love life, and the best thing they could do was teach the dogs to be happy when they were outside the bedroom, by shutting the door, giving it a second or two and rewarding them with praise and a little treat if they were quiet. Then they could gradually extend the time, before making it random – maybe a minute, maybe five minutes. That takes time and might be a bit of a passion killer in the early days, but it's worth the effort.

It's not uncommon for a dog (especially if they've just been rehomed and are unsure of their surroundings) to plant her flag in a corner of a sofa and defend it as if her life depended on it, perhaps by baring her teeth and growling.

People usually back off in that situation, which is understandable, but that just means the dog thinks the baring of teeth and growling worked and the behaviour gets worse. If you've got a dog who's getting a bit edgy on the sofa, she should lose that privilege, although that can be difficult to enforce. You've got to stick to your guns in an authoritative but calm way, and there's got to be something in it for them, perhaps a nice treat every time they get down and settle on the floor. Don't stand over them in a way that blocks their escape route: we all know what happens when we back a person or a dog into a corner . . .

Finally, I should add that if you're concerned or if the baring of teeth and growling spills over into something more aggressive, seek professional help.

Some dogs who take over the sofa aren't nervous, they're just being a bit bossy and possessive, in the same way they might be possessive over a bone. A possessive dog won't seem as quickfire-edgy as a nervy dog. You won't get the sense that they want to fight you; their manner will be more like a nightclub bouncer's: 'Mate, you're not coming on the sofa, and that's the end of it.'

When it comes to the sofa or bed, consistency is the most important thing. You can't be saying, 'I'll let you on the bed tonight because I'm feeling a bit down and need a cuddle,' and the next night saying, 'Get off! You're going in your crate,' because they won't know if they're coming or going.

I've already spoken about separation anxiety, and a dog wanting to get into bed with you isn't really that. But dogs can get a little bit antsy if you leave them at night, so maybe you should have a strategy to smooth things over.

We know that human bedtime routine is quite important in terms of setting you up for a good night's sleep, and it's the same for dogs. Dogs are creatures of habit, so every night before you go to bed, do the same things. Go for a walk or let her out in the garden to do her business. Maybe give her a bedtime treat – when our three dogs come in from the toilet, we chuck a treat on their beds, they scoff it and give us a look that says, 'I guess that's it for today?' That's when the lights go out and off we go to the Land of Nod.

If I have a bad night's sleep, I can be a bit grumpy the next day, or not thinking straight, and I'm convinced it's the same with dogs. So, if your dog's having an off day, seems a bit distant and isn't listening to you as normal, maybe it's because you both went to bed late the previous evening and you were both still wide awake when she normally would have been in bed. Food for thought?

If you're struggling at bedtime, what you definitely shouldn't do is lock your dog in the kitchen or utility room and let her cry and howl her head off. She may eventually get exhausted and collapse in a heap, but it won't be a pleasant experience for her (or indeed the neighbours!). Instead, try doing things in stages.

Getting a dog to stop sleeping in your bed if that's your choice can be a challenge, but if she's used to a crate and happy in it, maybe start the process by placing the crate in your bedroom and encouraging her to sleep in there. I should say that while we call them crates, to some dogs they're more like a cage. If they're not used to being in a crate and suddenly we bundle them into one, or maybe their only experience of being in one was at the vet or when they were scooped off the street, they're not going to like them one bit. But for other dogs, a crate can be the equivalent of a nice cosy den, especially if you put a blanket around it and plenty more bedding inside, plus something that smells of you, like an old sweatshirt. They'll still be able to hear your breathing from inside the crate, which they'll find reassuring, and as time goes on you can move the crate out of your bedroom bit by bit. It might take several weeks, but eventually they should be happily sleeping in the crate downstairs.

It's a good idea to put the crate somewhere that feels nice and secure, maybe a cubby hole under a work surface in the kitchen. Another trick you can use is dog-appeasing pheromone

(DAP), which is secreted by lactating dogs, and which you can now get in the form of sprays or plug-ins. People keep telling me they don't work, but my experience is that they can work in small, confined areas. If you're old enough to remember the 'Aah, Bisto!' adverts, that's basically how dogs feel when they smell DAP – pleasantly satisfied and relaxed.

If your dog doesn't like sleeping in crates, or it's too big for it to be convenient (if you've got a mastiff, that crate is going to take up a lot of room in your kitchen!), then you can still make a cosy area using a comfy dog bed.

Is my dog seeking attention?

I'm often asked if a dog is barking because they're trying to tell their owners something or they're just attention seeking. It's not always easy to tell the difference, but the thing to do is watch your dog very carefully while they're at it, because there are tell-tale signs.

Axel, one of my Rotties, had this big sonorous bark which he started to employ at the bay window whenever somebody was walking past. I didn't know as much then as I do now, so I thought he was barking to make people go away.

But one day, I was sitting on the sofa watching the telly, Axel ran towards the bay window and barked, and I wondered what would happen if I didn't go over to him to see what was out there as I usually did. So, instead of doing that, I resolutely ignored him while he barked himself hoarse. When he stopped barking for a couple of seconds, he looked around as if to say, 'Are you gonna come over or what?' (A dog's peripheral vision is very wide, incidentally – they can see behind them quite a long way – so even if they don't appear to be seeing you, they might be.) Then when I looked back at him, he started up again.

When I finally looked out of the window, there was nobody there, which was the eureka moment: Axel had learnt that if he barked at the bay window, whether there was somebody there or not, I'd get up off the sofa and – without thinking – give him a little tickle on the head, which was the attention he was craving. I needed to ignore his barking and wait for him to learn that it didn't work any more.

The other big clue was that my next-door neighbour said he was quiet when I wasn't there. In fact, he'd never heard Axel bark. That told me that he wasn't trying to get rid of people, he was just trying to get my attention.

When I suspect a dog is attention seeking, I ask the owners what they might be doing when it kicks off. Were they watching something on the telly? Were they engrossed in a book? Were they tapping away on their laptop? In other words, were they focused on something other than the dog?

I also ask how they react, and often it comes out that they're giving their dog attention when they think they aren't. Even if they're saying, 'Come on, please don't do that,' that's exactly what the dog wants, because any attention will be good attention to them.

Often, the best way to fix attention-seeking behaviour is just to ignore it. No talking, no eye contact, no stroking. Act as if the dog has ceased to exist. Some people seem to think you should fold your arms and turn around, but that's not really ignoring a dog, that's actually reacting to something they're doing. If you do that, the dog will think, 'OK, that's not what I had in mind, but at least it's something, it's a reaction, so I'll just carry on barking.' When your dog does stop barking, look over and say, 'Oh, good boy,' and eventually they'll make the connection: 'Huh, I get attention for being calm and doing nothing. I'll do that from now on.'

If your dog barks habitually in the middle of the night, even though he's been fed and put outside to go to the toilet, the worst thing you can do is get up and go to him. You'll just be making the problem worse by rewarding it and you'll be soothing him in the middle of the night forever.

The scientific term for ignoring unwanted attention seeking is 'behaviour extinction' – in other words, the behaviour becomes extinct over time if you don't reward it. Dogs aren't daft; they get bored of banging their head against a brick wall, just like humans. Eventually, they'll think, 'This is futile. I give up.'

But it's important to note that bad behaviour might take a long time to become extinct. You can get on the right track within a day, but it might be weeks before your dog truly sees the light. And you have to ignore the behaviour completely, not pick and choose, because that will lead you back to square one.

In addition, if you go down the ignoring route, it might be the case that the behaviour gets worse before it gets better. These are called 'extinction bursts', which make a lot of owners cave – maybe you'll be on a work Zoom and you'll give your dog a treat or a crafty stroke under your desk to keep them quiet, for example. But if you ride out the storm, peace will break out eventually.

If your dog is barking so incessantly that you're worried about getting in trouble with the council, the first thing you should do is knock on your neighbours' doors and explain the situation. Tell them that you're as concerned about the barking as they are, you're trying to fix it, but it might get a bit worse before things improve. Most neighbours will be OK with that.

Ignoring attention seeking is always my preferred route, but if you really don't think that's going to work with your neighbours, you may have to resort to Plan B, namely telling your dog off. Stand upright in an authoritative way (we look massive to dogs, as big as an old oak tree looks to us) and have a facial expression that conveys, 'No. I don't think so.' Your tone of voice shouldn't be nasty and shouty, but not pleasant, either. If they're barking at the window, you can try blocking (putting yourself between them and the window). If they calm down, even for a few seconds, switch everything the other way: give the dog a big, soppy smile, relax your body and say, 'Good boy, that's nice', in a gooey voice.

If you do go down the route of taking issue with your dog every time they bark, you've got to make sure your reaction can't be misconstrued as nice. So don't say stuff like, 'No, no, don't do that. Settle down, buddy', in a pleasant tone, because trying to calm down a dog while he's barking will make things worse, because it's still attention. The message from your body language and tone of voice needs to be, 'I know you're craving attention, but you're going about things the wrong way. I don't approve. If you're calm, though, I love that.' Dogs are pragmatic creatures. Once they figure that being calm and quiet is the key to getting the attention they desire, they'll ditch bark-ing pretty sharpish.

Occasionally though, I'll come across a dog whose attention seeking is so out of control that the obvious solution would be to have them rehomed. But it's rarely as simple as that, because the owner–dog bond can be so strong. I know it's a cliché, but some dogs really are a person's best friend.

Many years ago, long before I was on the telly, I met a guy called Shane who was in his twenties and had a Staffie called Sid. As soon as I walked in the house, I could see that there was a really strong bond between this guy and his dog. They clearly doted on each other and I soon found out why.

Shane explained that he literally owed his life to Sid. He'd been through a lot of mental health struggles, but Sid had given him a reason to get up every day and out in the fresh air. I'll always remember Shane saying to me: 'The thought of what would happen to Sid without me was enough to stop me doing something silly, if you know what I mean.' I knew what he meant, and I knew Sid would never leave Shane's side.

Shane's problem was that when Sid wasn't getting his full and undivided attention, he'd bark and howl. It didn't matter if it was in the house or outside, and it was causing Shane, and everyone around him, a lot of distress. He'd had a letter from the council saying that one of his neighbours had complained, and people would often tell him to shut Sid up when they were out and about. So as much as Shane owed his life to Sid, Sid was making his life unbearable.

Sometimes it's important for me to strip away the emotion from a story. It's not because I'm untouched by it, but in order to understand it properly, I have to look at it with my head and not my heart. And it soon became clear that Sid's attention-seeking behaviour was being rewarded.

Every time Sid started barking or howling, Shane would say, 'Come on, be a good boy', when he actually meant, 'Sid, you're being a naughty boy.' Worse, every time Shane said, 'Come on, be a good boy', all Sid heard was, 'Blah blah … good boy!' He sometimes got a stroke as well, because Shane was desperate to keep him calm. So the more Sid barked and howled, the more strokes and attention he got, and the more he kept doing it. Quite clearly, I needed to make sure that Shane only rewarded the good behaviour.

Provided you're on the right track in the first place (which is where I come in), doing the hard thing in the short term can have a big pay-off for everyone. So the first thing we did was knock on the neighbours' doors and say, 'Look, you might hear a bit more noise in the short term because we're going to ignore the dog's barking, but I promise it will fix things in the long term.' And by ignoring Sid when he barked and howled, he soon cottoned on that the quieter he was, the more likely he was to get the attention from Shane that he was craving. And by the end of the process, the bond was still as strong as before.

Why do dogs seem to dislike certain people?

There are some people who just rub dogs up the wrong way, bless 'em. They're not bad people, but they might not be dog people, which is often the problem.

Have you ever been in a room with somebody who's on edge and fidgety about something? Before you know it, you're feeling a bit on edge and fidgety yourself. It's the same with dogs: if your friend who's terrified of dogs comes round the house and your dog is a bit nervy anyway, that's not going to end well.

I once did a private consultation with a Chihuahua called Killer (I've changed the name to protect the innocent!) who was a bit nervous about people coming into the house and would bark and lunge at them.

Killer got used to me fairly quickly, probably because he worked out that his histrionics weren't going to make me flinch. But suddenly there was a knock on the door. 'Oh, it's the plumber,' said Killer's owner, 'I forgot he was coming round.' In walked the plumber, who was about six foot four and built like the proverbial outhouse. But it soon became apparent that while he could probably bench-press a small house, he was terrified of dogs, regardless of size.

As soon as Killer saw the plumber, he sprinted straight up to him and started barking. This poor man turned to stone and his eyes were wide as dinner plates. And when Killer jumped up at him, the plumber flung an arm forward (not to strike the dog, but just to defend himself) and that was it.

From that moment on, the dog hated him, all because of that one, probably involuntary, movement. The dog was thinking, 'I didn't really like you when you walked in, because you were a bit weird and stary. But when you started throwing your arms around like a maniac, that did it for me!'

Curing Killer's tendencies was clearly going to take some time, so for that morning we resorted to locking the plumber in the bathroom. Some dog behaviours take longer to fix than a leaking tap!

Paradoxically, the other kind of person nervous dogs are most likely to take exception to are ... wait for it ... dog lovers! Picture the scene: a dog lover knocks on the door of a house and the owner opens it and says, 'Look, she's a bit nervous and not very good with strangers. She won't hurt you, but she will bark, and she might growl a bit. So please just ignore her.' The dog lover says, 'Don't worry, I'm fine with dogs,' before strolling confidently in. The dog runs up to the dog lover and starts barking, the dog lover goes to stroke her on the head, and she nips him, at which point the owner says, 'Oh my God, she's never done that before ...'

But no one should be surprised that the dog lashed out. Put yourself in her shoes: she comes up to most people's shins and suddenly she's confronted with this gigantic specimen who's trying to stroke her with hands like shovels (to her, at least). Looked at in that way, her reaction makes perfect sense. In human terms, it would be like walking up to a stranger on the street, ruffling their hair and planting a big sloppy kiss on their cheek. That's not going to go down well.

Other no-nos when you meet a nervy dog for the first time are staring straight at them (threatening), bending over the dog, putting your face in theirs (terrible idea), making erratic movements and trying to hug them. Gesticulating wildly is another one, which makes you wonder how Italians get on with strange dogs.

A 2016 Hungarian study determined that dogs reacted less favourably to people with deep and/or angry-sounding voices than people with high-pitched, happy-sounding voices, but sometimes your dog might not like someone simply because they don't sound or look like you or anyone else in the family. Maybe they have a big beard, and they've never seen somebody with a big beard before, or they're wearing loads of jingle-jangling jewellery, and you're not very blingy.

Sometimes a dog's negative reaction to someone is to do with past trauma. And if it's a rescue dog, you probably won't know what that past trauma was. In some cases, dogs who were mistreated in the past will always distrust people who remind them of those terrible days. For example, you'll often hear about rescue dogs cowering around men, maybe because a man used to kick them, and hiding behind a woman's legs.

The famous dog behaviourist Patricia McConnell tells a story about a dog who welcomed most visitors but bit some. After some sterling detective work, it was discovered that everyone the dog had bitten had eaten pizza in the hours before visiting. It seems that a pizza delivery person had once kicked the dog, which is why they associated the smell of pizza with danger.

More common scents that dogs dislike include citrus, vinegar, mothballs (a nightmare if they ever time travel back to the 1970s), hairspray (ditto, except the 1980s), perfume and aftershave. And some dogs just get a bit narky if someone simply smells too different from their owner: a 2014 Emory University study showed that dogs develop a positive association with the scent of their closest human pal. No surprise?

Here's a strange one. Years ago, I visited a family of Jamaican heritage who had just taken in a rescue dog. About an hour into the consultation, the lady said to me, 'Can I ask you a slightly sensitive question?' I wondered what on earth was coming next . . . and then she said, 'Is it possible for a dog to be racist?'

As you can imagine, I was a little bit taken aback, and I told her that, no, I'd never come across a racist dog before. To which the lady said, 'I only ask because he doesn't seem to like anyone who isn't white.'

Despite the lady and her partner being Black, and their dog being OK with them, he had a bad habit of barking and lunging at Black people in the street, while ignoring anyone who was white. Now, this was tricky.

I asked about the dog's history and, as I suspected, the dog had been rescued from an isolated farm. This raised the possibility that he'd never seen a Black person until he was five, when his new owners took him in. After a wobbly start, he'd eventually got used to his new mum and dad, but when he was out walking, he was still slightly confused when he saw a Black person.

So, in answer to the lady's original question, clearly dogs aren't racist in the way humans are, in that they don't judge a person's character based on the colour of their skin – they've got far more sense than that – but they can be discombobulated by the unfamiliar, which can make them bark and lunge.

Is on or off the lead best?

I'd advise any dog owner to do some recall training, and not just at classes. Find a practice area that's safe for the dog and where you're not going to be a problem to anyone else if it goes wrong (maybe one of those dog fields that have sprung up all over the place), and don't even think about letting him off the lead in the outside world, with all its many distractions, until you've nailed it. Blind faith that your dog will come back isn't going to cut it.

It's not uncommon to see an owner walking along with their dog off its lead on a busy high street or next to a main road. What's the advantage of that? There isn't one. If your dog has been trained to walk happily beside you on a loose lead, there's no point in not having him on a lead. And not everybody likes dogs, so the sight of one coming towards them will make them nervous and uncomfortable. Plus, he's a dog, so just because he's never bolted across a road in six years, it doesn't mean he won't spot a squirrel one day and do exactly that, just as a giant articulated lorry is heading towards you. The only reason I can think of for doing that is if you want to show off: 'Look at me and my dog, strolling along together without a lead. Bet you can't do that . . .'

People whose dogs behave badly on the lead will sometimes say, 'We might as well just let him off.' That's fine if he's going to be a good boy, not bother other people and come back when you call him, but that's not always the case.

When I used to walk my two Rottweilers, they were pretty well behaved, as was I. But there was a guy in the village where I lived who had a real phobia of dogs – he'd see me and the two dogs coming towards him and freeze, with his arms held stiffly beside him and his eyes staring. After the first couple of times, I knew what was happening and started giving him a wide berth. Now imagine if that poor guy was at the park and my two

Rottweilers were off their leads. He's not going to care that I'm saying, 'Don't worry, mate, they're friendly!' He's going to be absolutely petrified. And dogs tend to be particularly interested in petrified people: 'Oh, that's weird, he's stopped moving. Let's go and check him out!'

Even if people aren't scared, they still might not appreciate the attention of one or more dogs. You wouldn't take your child to a park and say, 'Right, off you go. If there's somebody you want to play with, make them play with you. See that elderly couple over there on the bench, eating ice creams? Why don't you jump all over them and see if you can get the ice creams off them. They'll love it!' That would be considered bad parenting – but you see it with dogs.

As with a lot of topics, it depends on the dog and the situation. If you've trained your dog to come back and you're confident they're going to come back when you call them, then letting them off the lead is probably OK. But if you haven't trained them and/or you're not confident they're going to come back, letting them off the lead could end in disaster. I'll sometimes hear about people getting a rescue dog, letting them off the lead after just a couple of days and the dog scarpering, never to be seen again. Or attacking another dog: 'Oh sorry, I didn't know he'd do that.'

I once did a couple of videos about dog safety in the countryside for the National Farmers' Union, and the wise old sheep farmer said to me, 'A sheep is an animal with a great propensity to walk into a field and just die. For no apparent reason. It's a full-time job keeping the things alive, so I could do without people letting their dogs off the lead.'

A dog will think it's fun chasing a big woolly toy around, but even if they don't mean to do any harm, sheep can literally drop down dead from fright if a dog chases after them, and ewes can lose their lambs, which is why you see those signs on farms warning that sheep worrying is an offence – and those other signs warning that dogs doing the worrying will get shot.

The golden rule if you're anywhere near sheep or cattle is to keep your dog on a lead. Even if you're confident you can keep your dog under close control off the lead, you don't need to be showing off your heel work while walking across a field. Sheep will tend to move away anyway, but even if your dog is on a lead, give them as wide a berth as possible. And keep the noise down, because shouting and screaming at your dog will scare the sheep as well.

When I spoke to the cattle farmer, he told me he'd never met a farmer who hasn't got a story about people being trampled by cattle. I had that conversation in mind on a recent walk with a dog in the Cotswolds.

We'd done about six miles and I was thinking, 'I've bitten off a bit more than I can chew here,' because the Cotswolds are pretty hilly. Who knew? Then we came face to face with a field full of cows, some of them with calves.

Going back didn't really feel like an option, so I was just going to have to bite the bullet. As we walked along the footpath, these cows were staring straight at us, looking placid enough, as cows usually do. But who knows what's going on behind the eyes of a cow – maybe they were plotting my muddy demise? Plus, my companion was a Labrador seemingly crossed with a kangaroo, and what do dogs look like to cows? Predators.

Luckily, the cattle farmer I'd spoken to also had a few of his own golden rules. If you and your dog are on a footpath that runs across a field, most farmers would be happy for you to leave the footpath if it means not splitting a herd, or cows and their calves. And if a cow runs at you both, drop the lead or take your dog off it, because while cows are surprisingly fast – those cloven hooves are a bit like mud tyres on a 4x4 – they are rubbish at going around corners, whereas your dog can turn on a sixpence and outrun them. Once you reunite with your dog on the other side of the field, you can put him back on the lead.

What you do when a pig runs at you and your dog, I do not know. Although I did once train a New Zealand huntaway to herd pigs at a North Yorkshire farm. Jobs like that don't come up often!

I'm not a fan of letting dogs off the lead and allowing them out of sight for very long, for a variety of reasons. As well as livestock and wildlife considerations, there are plants that are poisonous to dogs (if you look up the list on the internet, it's surprisingly long, so you might also want to keep that in mind if you're a keen gardener). Mushrooms can also harm your dog if eaten, so if you're walking your dog in a woodland area and it's a bit damp, keep a close eye on him.

While we're on the subject of the countryside, you'll also find lots of sticks when you're out near woodland. Dogs famously love playing with these but the truth is, sticks aren't always fun and games.

Some dogs eat sticks rather than fetch them, which can cause an upset stomach (funnily enough, sticks aren't a recommended part of a dog's balanced diet). Dogs have also been known to get sticks stuck in their mouths or throats, and when you throw a stick for your dog, instead of landing flat, it can bounce in the wrong direction just as your dog goes to grab it, and go straight through their palate or the back of their throat. I'd recommend chucking a rubber toy with soft, round edges, instead.

Some dogs love sticks so much that once they've got one in their mouth, it's very difficult to remove them. Prevention is the best bet, which means good recall, so they don't pick up the stick in the first place. It's also where a good 'leave' command comes in handy. If your dog does go for a stick a couple of times, get him back on the lead, which will hopefully press the reset button. But if you do have to remove a stick manually, take your time, because the more you wrestle with him, the more it's a great big game and he'll get too excited to let go.

Something else dogs love about the countryside is rolling in poo. It doesn't matter whose poo it is – a badger's, a fox's, a goose's – some dogs adore the stuff, as if they were bathing in perfume or cologne.

It's said dogs roll in poo to disguise their scent, so they can creep on prey without them noticing. It's the smelly equivalent of camouflage. You might be thinking, 'But my Pomeranian isn't a predator,' and you'd be right. But all dogs were predators before humans came along to domesticate them. Nowadays, they probably don't even know why they're doing it, but that trait still exists deep within them, which is why it's so difficult to stop.

Dogs being very clever, they have a habit of rolling in poo while they're behind their owner, so try keeping your dog in front of you, so you can tell them 'No'. If they come away from the poo, praise them for it and maybe give them a treat, but don't lure them away with a treat after they've rolled in poo, because they'll think that's a bonus feature. And when you get your dog home, give him a good bath! (Why is it the smell of fox poo lingers so long? If the perfume companies could find out, they'd make a fortune ...)

Do dogs look like their owners?

The idea that owners look like their dogs sounds fanciful because, on the face of it, dogs don't look anything like humans. Unlike humans, dogs are covered in fur, have snouts, four legs and ears that flop around or stick up from the top of their heads. But studies suggest that similarities between dogs and their owners are real, as anyone who has seen a burly, shaven-headed bloke marching down the road with a bulldog would already have known.

Several studies have shown that people are able to match dogs with their owners simply by looking at photographs of their faces, at a rate much higher than chance. One study showed that owners with long hair are more likely to have dogs with long ears, while another study showed that heavier owners are more likely to have fatter dogs. A Japanese study even showed that dogs and their owners often have similar-shaped eyes, or at least eye regions.

All of this begs the question: why do owners get dogs who resemble themselves? According to the psychologist in charge of the Japanese study, it's because of a preference for the familiar. In other words, a dog will be a more comforting presence if it looks like us, and therefore other members of the family. That ties in with what we already knew about human evolution, in that we're more likely to seek out a mate who looks like us, in the hope that their genes will be compatible (one study even claims that humans choose cars that look like ourselves, which means that our cars often resemble our dogs!).

When I had Rottweilers, somebody pointed out one day that lots of things in my life were black and tan, including most of my wardrobe. They were right; I did dress myself like a Rott-weiler, and I didn't even realise it! My vehicle of choice at the time was an old-school Land Rover Defender. It had plenty of grunt and everything about it was robust and chunky. Rottie-like? You could say that.

So, yes, I think there's evidence, both anecdotal and scientific, that owners choose a dog that's like them, albeit subconsciously, and become even more like them over time.

Do dogs like babies?

When it comes to the wider discussion on babies and dogs, there are a couple of hard and fast rules: never leave them in a room together unsupervised; and even if you are in the room, never allow a dog near a baby if you have any doubt whatsoever about that dog's temperament.

Someone told me that a dog can move their head (and there-fore mouth) four times faster than a human can move their hand out of the way. I'm inclined to believe that, because I was once bitten by a German shepherd and the first I knew about it was when I felt the tug, and saw a tooth wound going right through my hand. So don't kid yourself that you'll be able to intervene if, God forbid, your dog does go for your baby.

However, I don't want to be alarmist, and there are lots of benefits of baby–dog relationships. For one, dogs certainly seem to make babies happy, as anyone who has seen any of the millions of baby–dog videos on the internet will know. But scientists' claims go way beyond that suggested by lots of babies giggling while being entertained by the family pooch.

Studies have also suggested that babies who grow up with dogs develop stronger immune systems, and are less likely to develop asthma, certain allergies and even obesity. Apparently, that's because gut bacteria linked to lower risks of allergic disease and leanness are significantly increased if there's a dog hanging around the house (I should add that babies can also be allergic to dogs, and that not everything a dog drags in will be good for your baby).

A study out of the University of Warwick revealed that some children view their relationship with their dog as more important than human relationships, and that they're more likely to confide secrets in their dog than humans. American research suggests that a pet dog can improve a child's cognitive development and empathy, and that children make fewer errors in cognitive tasks and memory tests if a dog is present. And a wide-ranging Australian study showed that dog ownership was associated with more active lifestyles and better social-emotional development (though it should be noted that even the scientists admit that not every child with a dog is better off than children without, because there are lots of other factors to take into account).

Perhaps you won't be surprised to learn that dogs, too, can benefit from being exposed to young humans early in their lives. Dr John Bradshaw, the eminent British animal behaviourist, says that if puppies haven't met any babies by the time they're about six months old, they can react quite badly when they do eventually meet one. He suggests that those latecomers to babies don't really recognise them as human, which makes sense, because babies are different to adult humans in lots of ways, from the noises they make to the way they smell.

One of the most common questions I'm asked is: 'How do we prepare our dog for the arrival of our first baby?' Well, the sooner you start the better, because things are about to change in your house, big time. And two of the biggest changes for your dog are that she's going to be getting less attention and potentially barred from areas she was previously allowed to enter.

Start by creating little bits of separation, so if you're at home, let her chill out on her own in another room, maybe just for half an hour at first. If she's one for attention seeking – 'Play with this! Play with this!' – resist the temptation, because you won't always be able to play when the baby arrives. It doesn't mean you no longer love her; you just need to get the message across that you need some 'you' time, which will soon become 'you and baby' time.

To keep her entertained, you might want to give her some engrossing, calming toys, such as a rubber Kong toy that you can put food inside or something they can gnaw on (dried yak milk chews are a great bet – they last for ages and can also help clean your dog's teeth). What you don't want to give them is anything they can fling all over the room, which will get them revved up.

You might want to make some areas of the house off-limits. If she is allowed upstairs, maybe now is time to install a baby gate on the bottom step. Failing that, watch her like a hawk and whenever she puts one paw on the step, tell her no. And when she comes away, tell her what a good girl she is. The same principle applies to the sofa – if she has always been allowed up there, it might be time to tell her that from now on, it's invite only, because you'll likely appreciate a little sanctuary for you and your baby from time to time.

Maybe just before you bring the baby into the house for the first time, let your dog smell a blanket the baby's been swaddled in, to get her used to the smell. But don't just give it to your dog and go straight off to do something else, otherwise there's a chance she'll start ragging it all over the room. That's not really an association you want to be making. Instead, sit down, let her smell the blanket and tell her what a good girl she is for being calm.

When the baby arrives, do things in stages and split responsibilities. For what follows, I'm assuming your dog has never shown any signs of aggression and that you are able to physically hold your dog back if she's too inquisitive. Preferably when your baby is asleep (you don't want him to spook the dog with any strange noises!), and while your dog's on a lead, let them have a sniff of the general area, but keep their nose about six inches away initially. Then, as time goes by, allow them to get a bit nearer. And don't make a big deal of it, act as if it's all perfectly normal. Which, I suppose, it is.

It's best to try to keep your dog's routine pretty much the same as it was, particularly with regards exercise. Dare I say it, you might even want to give your dog more exercise than before. I know that's not easy with a new baby, when you're busier and more tired than you've ever been, but it will mean your dog is more likely to be calmer around the house.

Older kids usually fall into two categories when it comes to dogs: the excitable 'Dog! Dog! Dog!' kids who can't wait to stroke a dog; and kids who are nervous around them.

Excitable children and their sudden movements and loud noises can spook a dog and set him off, while dogs can be a bit funny around nervous children. Either way, the golden rule whenever a child meets a dog is to ask, 'Is it OK if he/she says hello?' Then get the child to extend the back of their hand and wait for the dog to come to them. If you're the dog owner, calmness is key. If you're too excited, it will create excitement in the child and anxiety in the dog, which is a bad combination.

When it comes to slightly more grown-up kids, it's best to get them involved with training as early possible. Obviously, I don't mean tasking your seven-year-old with taking your dog to classes – that wouldn't be wise – I just mean making sure everyone is consistent when it comes to commands.

There's a good chance that if you're clear and consistent with your commands, the kids will pick them up from you, whereas if you're not clear and consistent, you've got no chance of anyone else mastering them. Sometimes I'll hear from an owner who had all the commands down pat, until the kids started giving different commands and confusing the dog.

The most common command that gets mixed up is 'down'. I've lost count of the number of times I've seen a dog lie down on the sofa when someone has told him '(get) down', because he's used to 'down' meaning 'lie down' (and thinks the command for getting down from the sofa is 'off').

You also need to teach your kids not to be too rough with a new puppy, or indeed too cuddly. You want your puppy to get used to being handled, but we've all heard about dogs nipping children when they've been tormented or hugged too tight and felt restricted. And if your puppy does nip at one of your children, don't make a big deal of it. If everyone starts screaming and shouting, the dog could get more and more edgy and switch to fighting mode.

Is my dog a wolf?

No. And yes. Confused? Don't worry, lots of people are.

Our domestic dogs (scientific name *Canis familiaris*) are classed separately in biology from wolves (*Canis lupus*). They are from the same group, or genus (Canis = canines), but a different species (familiaris = domestic/family dog, while lupus = wolf). And yet, we all know that our pet dogs evolved from wolves of one kind or another – the scientific consensus is that the domestic dog's wolf ancestors are now extinct – but no one knows for sure whether domestication started in Europe, the Arctic or Asia, or indeed when the process kicked off. Some say about 10,000 years ago, others 30,000 years ago, which is quite a gap.

We'll never know for certain exactly what early domestication looked like – there aren't many cavemen still around whom we could ask – but one theory is that wolves were attracted to hunter-gatherer camps by the smell of cooking meat and discarded bones. These wolves would have been the least fearful (and least fear-aggressive) from their pack, which made them less wary around humans and better bets for further domestication. It wouldn't have taken the humans long to work out that these proto-dogs came in quite handy around the place, because they could alert them to the approach of potential attackers and defend them from competing predators during and after a hunt.

Oxford University archaeologist and geneticist Greger Larson believes humans domesticated dogs twice, his theory being that way back in the mists of time, somewhere in western Eurasia, humans were forming close bonds with wolves, at roughly the same time as humans were doing the same thing further east.

According to Larson, during the Bronze Age, some of the eastern dogs migrated westward with their new human chums, mated with the western dogs and effectively replaced them. (I should add that not all of his fellow academics are convinced – some of them think those western 'dogs' might actually have been wolves.)

Nobody disputes that these early, proto-dogs were more wolf-like than dog-like, but whenever someone says to me, 'A dog is basically a wolf,' I always reply, 'Anyone who thinks that has never lived with a wolf.' Thirty to forty thousand years isn't long in evolutionary terms – in fact, it's barely the blink of an eye – but human intervention supercharges the process, and that fluffy little thing that sits on your lap on the sofa every night is very far from the wolves you see on wildlife programmes, howling and tearing deer apart.

We've got a rough idea of how selective breeding by humans might have changed wolves into dogs because of a famous Russian experiment that has been going on for the last 70 years, although with silver foxes instead of wolves. By selectively breeding less fearful foxes together, sure enough, within a few generations, tamer foxes were being born. They were also behaving more like dogs, and their fur started changing colour. They were still silver foxes, but if the experiment goes on for hundreds of years, maybe we'll have to start calling them something else.

However, while that fluffy little thing in your house definitely isn't a wolf, they're pretty much the same internally. They've got the same organs arranged in the same way (although wolves have larger brains), and the same number and arrangement of teeth (28 in puppies, 42 in adults), although a wolf's fangs are far longer and its molars more adapted for crushing bone.

Which brings us to diet. You often hear people say, 'If dogs aren't that much different to wolves, in terms of physiology, they should eat the same as wolves do.' That's how a lot of raw food is marketed, and it's true that wolves are overwhelmingly carnivorous. They might eat the odd berry, but they'll mainly be hunting and eating everything from bison to insects. But scientists are still arguing as to whether dogs are carnivores or omnivores (dogs certainly have different genes that enable them to utilise grains), so I wouldn't feel bad about feeding your dog dry food, as long as it's good stuff.

I fed my two Rottweilers raw food for over ten years, chicken carcasses with other nutrients mixed in. The boys did well on it, but it was a heck of a faff, so now I buy good-quality commercial food. I'm not a dog nutritionist, but I think it's safe to say that, as with human food, you usually get what you pay for.

My advice is to forget about the glossy packaging and focus on the ingredients. And while you see a lot of grain-free products nowadays, most dogs are just fine eating them (although grains are known to make dogs prone to flatulence). Incidentally, I had a chat recently with a veterinary cardiologist who advised against a grain-free diet for Scooby, our boxer who has a heart condition. By all accounts, the jury is still out as to whether grain-free is suitable for all dogs. If you're in doubt, have a chat with your vet.

Not so long ago, a lot of dogs would mainly eat what their owners ate – everyone's got stories about their grandparents giving their dogs leftovers or Mars Bars – but we know a lot more than we did back then, and a lot of foods that humans eat are poisonous to dogs, chocolate being the classic example. Raisins and grapes are also a no-no, and garlic and onion can be problematic in large quantities. And you don't want to put a saucer of tea down, because caffeine isn't good for dogs, and some tea contains other harmful ingredients such as theobromine and tannins, which can cause vomiting and diarrhoea.

Dogs being individuals, different ones can be allergic to different things, so it's often a case of trial and error. But the last bit of your sausage sandwich on a Sunday morning or a little corner of Cheddar is unlikely to do any harm.

Are dogs born or made?

Years ago, I posed this question on my Facebook page: 'Dog behaviour, nature or nurture?' I let it roll all weekend and there were people arguing vociferously on both sides. The truth is, all of us, humans and dogs, are products of nature *and* nurture.

I never knew my grandad on my mum's side but, as I grew up, I started to come out with some of the same mannerisms as him, which suggests they were coded in my DNA. Obviously, nurture made me different to my granddad in other ways but, in raising me, my parents were working with many of the same raw materials. A lot of dog training works on similar lines, in that you're working around certain genetic tendencies, which might be inconvenient.

I sometimes rather facetiously say to terrier owners, 'If your dog could write a CV, it would say: 'Can work underground without supervision; can go into the lair of other animals, kill them and drag out their dead bodies, etc.' It's not the nicest way to talk about your pet dog, but it describes precisely what some were bred to do. And it's quite different to the job description for the perfect pet.

There has been some truly remarkable science done to work out where all these different breeds came from, from your giant Saint Bernard to your tiny Chihuahua. We already knew that our human ancestors started the process of selective breeding thousands of years ago, by picking out the best hunters, guards, herders and companions, but until recently we didn't know how and when most of these breeds came into being.

For 20 years, geneticists from the National Human Genome Research Institute in Bethesda, Maryland, collected DNA samples from dogs of all shapes and sizes, and by 2017 they had a database of almost 1,500 dogs representing 161 breeds (there are about 350 pedigree breeds, although people argue about the exact number). From this database, they were able to build a family tree and group dogs with similar traits together – herders, guarders, companions, spaniels, mastiff-like breeds, terriers, retrievers, scent hounds, sight hounds and spitz breeds (such as huskies and, surprisingly, corgis). These quite large groups with common ancestries suggested that ancient humans were selecting dogs for specific purposes, but that it was only in the last 200 years that many of our modern breeds were created.

Some breeds were employed specifically to create new ones, such as the pug, which was brought to Europe from China to miniaturise other breeds (thus, if you've got a toy dog, it may be shot through with pug DNA). Mixing and matching also meant that certain defective genes were passed on, knowledge of which will help vets diagnose potential genetic problems shared by breeds that were previously thought not to have much in common.

Various studies have already told us about a dozen breeds that were genetically divergent and distinctive from modern breeds, including the chow-chow, the Shar-Pei, the saluki, the Afghan hound and the New Guinea singing dog (which 'yodels' instead of barking). And what all this rich history adds up to is a whole lot of dogs who do things in lots of different ways.

It's just in some dogs' natures to be triggered by certain things. It's why when your dog sees a squirrel, it will bark the house down and scratch maniacally at the French doors, and will still be doing it after the squirrel has disappeared. When they saw that squirrel, something in their mind clicked, and all they wanted to do was catch that squirrel, even though most modern dogs haven't got a snowball's chance in hell of succeeding.

Can you train around these natural triggers? Can you tweak certain behaviours? Yes, and it's often quite surprising what changes you can make. But it might not always be easy, in the same way as it might not be easy to train a Yorkshireman to be less outspoken. (As a Yorkshireman myself, I'm allowed to say that. You can always tell a Yorkshireman, but you can't tell him much!)

I liken variations in dog breeds to variations in people from different regions. When you're on the Tube in London, nobody even looks at each other, and God forbid you do the northern thing and say hello to someone, for mass panic is likely to ensue. But if you're standing at a bus stop in Sheffield, people think it's odd if you don't say hello.

Of course, you might be on the Tube one day and strike up a lovely conversation with the smiley Londoner sitting opposite you, just as the scowling Yorkshireman at the bus stop in Sheffield might tell you where to go. So while people from different regions *tend to* have certain traits, there are overlaps, and it's the same with different dog breeds.

There are obviously breed tendencies, which is why we don't use Pomeranians as guard dogs, and you wouldn't necessarily get a Shar-Pei if you wanted a lap dog (Shar-Pei were bred in China as guard or fighting dogs). But, like humans, dogs are individuals, which means your Pomeranian might behave more like a lion and seemingly want to kill everything that moves, and your Shar-Pei might be a real sweetheart who wants cuddles all the time.

Genetics is like a fruit cake: you can put icing on it to make it look like a sponge cake, but you can't remove or rearrange the raisins, so it's now a fruit cake with icing on top. In the same way, owners have to accept that they're working with a set of dispositions that have been bred into their dogs over hundreds of generations, whether it's a spaniel that was bred to flush out and retrieve birds, a terrier that was bred to catch rats or a husky that was bred to pull sleds.

Is my dog just daft?

Back in 1994, Stanley Coren, a former professor of psychology at the University of British Columbia, released a book called *The Intelligence of Dogs*, which explained his theories about the differences in intelligence between dog breeds and even went as far as to rank them, with Border collies taking top spot and Afghan hounds propping up the table (sorry, Afghan owners).

As you can imagine, Professor Coren's book ruffled a few feathers (funnily enough, people didn't want to be told that their dog wasn't the sharpest tool in the box), and some researchers have rubbished his methodology, but his ranking has come to be widely accepted as a good rough guide to a breed's trainability.

However, there will be variations within any given breed, and very occasionally I'll come across a collie who should have worn one of those pointy dunce hats to puppy training and a Pekingese who would have been a *Mastermind* contender were he human.

Given that most modern dogs are kept purely as pets, it doesn't really matter if your pooch doesn't seem to be as bright as Professor Coren suggests he should be. Manchester terriers were bred to catch vermin in the 19th century, but if your Manchester terrier brought a rat in from the garden you probably wouldn't be happy, because his job nowadays is to be cute, mild-mannered and like a fuss – though a sheep farmer with a slower-than-expected collie who keeps splitting the flock will obviously have a different perspective.

Besides, intelligence doesn't necessarily equate with goodness. And, of course, there are different kinds of intelligence. For example, the intelligence of a collie, which was bred and trained to herd (which means thinking fast and being quick on their feet) is different to the intelligence of a Rottweiler.

Having had a couple of Rotties, I'm biased, but my experience is that they're deep-thinking dogs. I once read a story about a burglar who sneaked around the back of a house and put his hand through the letterbox, to try to open the door. Unfortunately for him, there was a female Rottweiler inside who bit into his arm and wouldn't let go. He eventually got his arm back, but only after a lot of damage had been done, and he ended up getting arrested because of DNA they found in his blood, which was all over the kitchen floor. I guess he was already having a bad day when the police came knocking!

A lot of dogs in that situation would have barked and barked before the guy had put his arm through the letterbox, but it's typical for a Rottie to sit there and think, 'This is odd. Who's this coming? I don't normally hear a sound like that. Oh, what's this? An arm through the door. I need to act . . .'

Another Rottie story I love came from a police sergeant who used to head up his constabulary's dog section. He explained that while German shepherds would do what he asked them to do unquestioningly – and do it over and over – Rotties were quite different.

So, having trained a German shepherd to find someone who was hiding, this police sergeant would say, 'Go find', and she'd go off, not find anyone, come back, and he'd be able to tell her to do it again. But when he had a Rottie for a while, he'd say to her, 'Go find', so he'd go off, not find anyone, come back – then when he told him to do it again, he'd just sit there and look at him, as if to say, 'Pointless! There's nothing there, boss. You know that; you just saw me look.'

This guy's colleagues were all calling his Rottie stupid – and, admittedly, his behaviour wasn't ideal for police work – but who's the more intelligent really? The dog who keeps doing the same thing over and over, expecting different results, or the dog who quickly works out that nothing's doing?

What all dogs have in common is that they usually, although not always, learn from trial and error and aren't so good at conditional thinking. That means they're unable to imagine the consequences of doing something stupid, like running in front of a car. In contrast, adult humans don't need to have been hit by a car to know it's a bad idea to run in front of one.

When should we say goodbye?

Dogs will often tell you when enough is enough. You'll get up one morning, look at your dog in her bed and she'll give you a look that says, 'I don't want to get up now. I don't want to get up at all. I just want to go back to sleep.'

That was the case with my first Rottweiler, Axel. It was very sad, but it was clear he'd made the decision to call it a day. He had a heart condition, so he was getting short of breath and tired all the time. We kept him comfortable, but one day he was almost unresponsive. He may have raised his eyebrows slightly, but the message was clear: 'No, sorry. I don't want to do anything. Just let me lie here.' That was when I knew the time had come.

But it varies from dog to dog. For example, a vet once said to me, 'I had a spaniel who lived for a ball, and I always thought, "The day he stops wanting to chase one, I'll know that's it, because there'll be no quality of life left."'

Then there was a lady I spoke to recently whose dog had canine cognitive dysfunction (CCD) – doggy dementia. The poor thing lost control of her bladder and bowels. The dog had always hated being showered, and now she was being showered several times during the day and night, even at three o'clock in the morning. She was blind but wouldn't have known where she was even if she could see. I thought, 'This dog might not be in physical pain, but she's stressed during the day, and she's stressed during the night. Where's the quality of life?'

Gordon, Axel's 'brother from another mother', didn't know when to quit. He was very poorly with brain cancer, which was affecting him in all sorts of ways. It was making him a bit off-balance, and I don't think he could see straight, because he kept bumping into things. I think he was in pain, and while we were doing our best to manage it, I sometimes wonder if we could have read the signs earlier.

One day, he was walking around the garden, trying to work out where he was going, but he still had this determined air about him: 'I'll be all right in a minute. Don't you worry, I'll shake this off ...' – but I had to say to him, 'You won't be all right, mate, you're never going to shake this off.' And I made the awful decision for him.

I mentioned our Patterdale terrier, Tish, previously. As well as being blind, she's starting to show signs of CCD.

Sometimes, she doesn't seem to know where she is. Before we moved, on occasion I'd find her in the hallway, frozen to the spot. When she first started doing it, I put it down to her blindness, but blind dogs are usually pretty good at navigating their own houses. Other times, she seemed unsettled and would pace up and down, making an anxious 'meeping' sound. At first, I thought it might have been the hot weather that was bothering her, but she carried on doing it into the autumn.

Signs of dementia in dogs include: anxiety and restlessness; irritability and aggression; getting lost in what should be familiar surroundings; not recognising old friends and family members (including other pets); altered sleeping patterns (maybe sleeping more during the day and being awake at night); and forgetting previously learnt training, including toilet training.

As I write, autumn has turned to winter and Tish certainly doesn't have all those symptoms, but that's often why CCD is difficult to diagnose, because it creeps up on dogs and many of the signs, taken individually, are common in elderly dogs. We're monitoring her carefully.

A few years ago, I worked with a greyhound called Clara who had suddenly started, according to her owners, being very disobedient. She'd bark at night, wanting to be let out in the garden, she'd wee in the house, ignore commands, and even threaten to bite anyone who went near her while she was in 'her' corner of the sofa. In fact, Clara hadn't shown any affection for weeks. It was all very out of character.

Clara was only nine, but she ticked all the CCD boxes. So sadly, I had to tell the family that there was nothing I could do to 'fix' things. As with Alzheimer's, there's no cure, although interventions can be made if it's spotted early, including supplements and specialist drugs which may slow the development and improve quality of life (there's also evidence that dogs whose brains have been well exercised throughout their lives, with training and games, are less likely to get CCD). But in Clara's case, she'd become a shell of the nice friendly dog she once was, living as she was in a scary world she couldn't understand. She had very little quality of life left and her owners took the sad, but I think right, decision to have her put to sleep.

It's not at all surprising that people find making that decision difficult, because dogs really do become part of the family. For as long as they're around, they're with us every step of the way. And they depend on us for everything. I know it's a cliché, but dogs are almost like children, so it's a bitter blow when they start to slip away. But the dog's quality of life is the most important thing, and we must think about what's best for them, not what feels best for us. Your dog will have given you so much joy, and perhaps the most loving thing you can do in return is decide when to say goodbye.

* * *

Make no bones about it, dogs are smart cookies (excuse the mixed dog-treat-related metaphor!). But the world they inhabit has changed beyond all recognition since they first became man's best friend, so they need a bit of assistance to make it through the day.

Luckily, we humans have been learning to help for a long time, so it's almost second nature. And it's not as if dogs aren't doing their bit. Not that they have to do much – sometimes just a well-timed nuzzle can help us through our day too. We look after each other, dogs and people. It's a very special partnership.

Chapter 4

How Dogs Perceive the World

Dogs navigate the world armed with a formidable arsenal of senses. In fact, in a senses head-to-head with humans, it's a pretty close-run thing.

Dogs have a far more powerful sense of smell than humans (though they still lag behind horses, mice, cows, rats, bears and – surprise, surprise – elephants), and also outrank us when it comes to hearing, although we are both mid-table in that respect. Humans have a more sophisticated sense of taste than dogs (catfish come out top in that category, in case you were wondering), and better vision overall. But here's my caveat: I suspect we don't understand the full extent of a dog's powers because we judge their senses based on what we know of our own, and I reckon there are one or two we have no idea about.

Think of it this way: if you were speaking to an alien who didn't have a concept of smell, how would you describe it? You couldn't, could you? And it might be the same with dogs, in that they have secret senses they'll never be able to describe to us.

But while humans can do without knowing anything about these secret senses, we do need to know how dogs experience their surroundings in other ways, so that we can keep them healthy, happy and safe. If we don't try to understand what scares dogs, or gets them too excited, or how much exercise they should be getting, and a thousand and one other things, we could be making life harder for them than it needs to be.

How powerful are dogs' noses?

A dog's sense of smell is its most potent (known!) weapon, far more powerful than a human's. Dogs have about 40 times more smell-sensitive receptors than us (the average for a dog is about 225 million, but bloodhounds have about 300 million), and their sense of smell is thought to be about 40 times more sensitive than a human's. If that wasn't amazing enough, dogs also have moveable nostrils that help them work out where a smell is coming from, and they smell in 'stereo', that is they smell separately with each nostril.

Their nose is therefore extremely high spec, but in reality it's just the piece of apparatus that collects the data, and the actual processor is even more impressive. As a proportion of the whole brain, humans have a larger visual cortex than dogs (the visual cortex is responsible for processing visual information), while a dog's brain has a much larger olfactory cortex (which is responsible for processing smells). No wonder people often say that dogs 'see' the world through their noses. On that note, a 2022 study by Cornell University suggested that a dog's sense of smell is integrated with its sense of sight via the brain's olfactory and occipital lobes.

A dog's olfactory experience is a lot richer than ours, and they'll be picking up lots of smells we're not. Scientists even believe that a dog can separate smells out, so if a dog walks into your kitchen while you're cooking, she won't just be thinking, 'Hmmm, smells like lasagne tonight', she will be thinking, 'Right, what have we got here … minced beef, half cooked … notes of olive oil … I'm also getting tomatoes, tinned … oh, and hints of parsley …'.

I'm just postulating, but I reckon if we could talk to a dog, she'd tell us that her ability to separate aromas was a bit like a human's ability to separate different sounds within a piece of music, such as guitar riffs, vocals and basslines.

The reason dogs have such a cracking sense of smell comes down to survival. Like most animals, wild canines need their noses to sniff out food and mates and avoid predators, and the domestic dog never lost that incredible ability, despite having humans to rely on. It's why our blind Patterdale terrier Tish is still going, and you even get functioning dogs who are deaf and blind.

I've lost count of the number of times a couple has said to me, 'Our dog knew we were pregnant before we did.' These dogs would stay very close to Mum at all times, as well as sniffing her tummy. Scientists can't say for sure whether dogs know a baby is on the way or not, but it's likely they know something different is going on, because a pregnant woman's chemistry changes, which in turn can lead to a change in odours.

Famously, dogs can also be trained to use their noses to detect lots of different health conditions, including cancer, malaria and diabetes (although, it should be noted, there are sceptics in the medical world), as well as drugs, explosives, leaking pipes, rhino poachers, and many things besides. And as I've already discussed in a previous chapter, dogs are also able to detect different human emotions with their nose, including fear and happiness.

There's nothing unusual about your dog stopping and sniffing every few yards on a walk, especially if you've got a scent hound, such as a beagle or a foxhound. And lots of people seem to believe that because their dogs have this very intense olfactory world, they should never stop their dog from sniffing. However, the problem with never stopping your dog from sniffing is that it's a very rewarding behaviour, especially for scent hounds, and any behaviour that's rewarding can become obsessive, just like humans and drugs.

Someone recently contacted me about their Labrador, whose sniffing had become so all-consuming his recall had gone out of the window. Every time they went for a walk, his nose would be glued to the ground, and when his owner tried to shift him, he'd dig his heels in. He was probably thinking something along the lines of, 'This. Is. Fascinating. I'm getting some pigeon ... some kid ran past yesterday ... oh, and a baby ... there's an old kebab over there ... RABBIT! RABBIT! RABBIT!' I always imagine that dogs like that can almost *see* the aroma, like the visible wafts you used to see in old cartoons.

The owner of this Labrador needed to take back control. She needed to teach her dog that there will be times during the walk when he absolutely can have a sniff, but for most of the walk, she's in charge. Her attitude needed to be, 'Right, *I'm* going out for a lovely walk, and you are coming with *me*.'

If you have an obsessive sniffer who won't budge, adopt a 'this is non-negotiable' demeanour. Don't try to drag him away from whatever he's smelling, because the more you pull in one direction, the more he'll pull in the other. That's where the little lead flicks you might have seen me do on the telly come in – done properly, without force, it doesn't do the dog any harm; it's just a slight nudge in the right direction if he hesitates. If he moves, tell him what a good dog he is, and hopefully you'll eventually regain control and he'll also respond to recall when he's off-lead.

Can dogs see well?

While your dog's sense of smell is king, their eyesight isn't bad either.

For a long time, it was widely accepted that dogs saw in shades of black and grey and could only make out the general shape of things. But when scientists were able to compare the structure of the canine and human eye, they discovered that wasn't the case at all.

Canine eyes have a larger lens and corneal surface, as well as more rods in the retina and a reflective membrane, both of which enhance night vision. Those findings led scientists to conclude that ancestors of the domestic dog were nocturnal hunters, who relied on movement to track and catch their food in the dark. You may have been out for a walk with your dog at dusk, seen a rabbit in the distance and thought, 'I can't believe he's not seen that.' It's thought that dogs have 20/75 vision (whereas perfect human sight is rated 20/20 on the same scale), which means objects tend to become more blurry the further away they are for dogs – so in that sense, we have sharper sight than them. Wait until the rabbit moves, though, and he'll lock on like a laser beam.

Dogs also have a very wide field of vision. We can see almost 180 degrees horizontally (if you put your arms out to the side, like you're flying, you can't quite see your hands). Dogs, meanwhile, can see up to 240 degrees horizontally, depending on the shape of the dog's skull and the position of its eyes. It's almost like they've got rear-view mirrors, which obviously comes in very handy for wild canines who hunt and need to keep an eye out for predators.

Scientists also believe that a dog's colour vision is broadly similar to that of somebody with red–green colour blindness. There are websites and apps that allow you to see the world as your dog sees it, and you'll find that they see a lot of things in a grainy, greyish brown, almost like a very old film. For this reason, when you buy your dog a ball, avoid orange or red and get him a yellow or blue one instead, because he'll be able to distinguish those colours from green grass.

Believe it or not, you can buy glasses for dogs – 'doggles', as they're called – but they're really to protect against dust, debris or sand. Brachycephalic dogs with bulgy eyes are the main breeds to benefit from these contraptions, because they're more vulnerable to eye injuries, or those exposed to a strong sun. Dogs who live at high altitude, where there is more ultraviolet light, can develop pannus, which is an inflammatory condition of the cornea, and they can also develop cataracts.

If you're worried that your dog's eyesight might be failing – maybe they've started bumping into things when you take them to unfamiliar places – take them to the vet. But remember, even if they do have a problem with one or more eye, they've got their very powerful sense of smell to fall back on.

Are a dog's ears just for hearing?

So, humans pip dogs when it comes to sight, but a dog's hearing is better than ours in many ways.

Human babies can hear from the moment they're born, while puppies enter the world with their ear channels closed. However, their ears open after a couple of weeks, and after about 20 days they can hear as well as an adult dog.

A dog's sensitivity to low-pitched sounds is much the same as a human's, but dogs are able to hear sounds that are higher in pitch than humans can, including ultrasounds produced by rodents and insects (probably because they would have eaten things like mice, rats and voles pre-domestication). That's why your dog sometimes looks like he can hear something that you can't.

Some dog trainers use ultrasonic whistles for this reason, and it might also explain why dogs respond more to high-pitched voices. In 2023, Hungarian researchers published a study that showed that dogs show greater brain sensitivity to words spoken by women than men, suggesting that dogs are more responsive to the exaggerated intonation and stress of the typical female voice. Most dog trainers already suspected this, which is why you'll often hear them speaking to dogs in a higher-pitched, sing-song voice, as if they're speaking to an infant. Incidentally, smaller dogs are more sensitive to higher-frequency sounds because of their smaller heads and their proportionally bigger ears.

Talking of high-pitched sounds, I once worked with a German shepherd who hated the beeping that traffic lights made. In fact, it drove him so mad that he'd jump up and try to bite the box with the button on that the sound came out of. I reckon that if he could have spoken, it probably would have been solely expletives. And it just kept getting worse, because he thought it was his biting that was making the noise stop. It took a lot of repetition (I haven't crossed the same road so many times in my life), but by rewarding him whenever he *didn't* react to the sound, he became much calmer. Often, we forget to praise a dog for doing nothing, when ironically 'nothing' is essentially what we wanted all along.

The superior amplification abilities of the small bones in a dog's inner ear means they can hear quieter sounds than humans. According to the experts, some dogs can hear sounds that are four times quieter than a human can hear – even termites in a wall and the inner workings of digital gadgetry.

In addition, dog ears contain 18 muscles, which allow them to swivel in different directions, like a satellite dish. They can also move each ear independently of the other one, which helps them work out where sounds are coming from.

We know that human hearing can be damaged by loud sounds, which is why we wear ear protection in certain noisy environments. And while we don't know how much a noise a dog can take, it's speculated that a dog's hearing could be damaged at lower levels of noise than humans because their hearing is more sensitive. Some dogs used by the US military even wear ear defenders!

Most owners like to sit on the sofa massaging or scratching their dogs' ears, and a 2019 study by Washington State

University revealed that any kind of dog petting can significantly reduce stress levels in humans. But most dogs will be particularly appreciative of a good rub of the old jug handles because their ears are packed with sensitive nerve endings (the only other parts of a dog that are anywhere near as sensitive are their tummies and the bits between their toes). When these nerves are stimulated, they send signals through the body that release endorphins, otherwise known as the feel-good chemical – that's why your dog might close her eyes and fall asleep while you're doing it. I should add that not all dogs like having their ears rubbed and it's important not to force it. Try giving her belly a good scratch instead!

As you've no doubt noticed, different breeds have different-shaped ears, and that's down to selective breeding by humans. Upright ears are the most natural, and any other shapes were often bred into a dog for practical reasons. A Jack Russell's ears stand upright but fold halfway to protect the inner ear, because that particular breed was designed to dig foxes out of their burrows, while it's thought that a basset hound's pendulous ears 'catch' scent molecules and direct them to their nose, making them track more effectively.

Dogs also communicate with their ears. If a dog meets another dog and his ears are pointed straight up, he's probably excited and/or wants to play. More generally, pricked ears signal that a dog is alert, engaged in an activity or intrigued by something, while if your dog's ears are shifted slightly back, they're probably feeling nervous.

Flattened or pinned ears can signal submission, especially if combined with a submissive body posture (owners often report that their dogs pin their ears back after doing something naughty, like tipping a bin over), but if they're pinned as flat as they can possibly go, they're likely to be scared and entering fight-or-flight mode. If you're out and about and your dog's ears are moving all over the place, like an out-of-control radar system, there's probably a lot happening around them and they're trying to work out what on earth is going on.

You might be wondering how dogs with particularly floppy ears, like basset hounds, communicate with them. Well, we have to assume that they can't to any great degree, but that doesn't mean they can't communicate at all, just like dogs without tails.

Dogs are very good at picking up on the tone of a human's voice or noises, in the same way a human friend might recognise how you're feeling from the first few words of a phone conversation and say, 'Are you OK?'

In a 2020 American study, researchers looked at how dogs reacted when their owner or a stranger pretended to laugh or cry. The dog gave more attention to the criers than the laughers, and when the stranger cried, the dog showed higher levels of stress.

And a Hungarian study from 2014 showed that the canine brain reacts to voices in much the same way the human brain does. Researchers trained dogs to lie still and relaxed in an MRI scanner and discovered that emotionally charged sounds, such as crying and laughter, elicited similar responses as in humans. Their brains also showed similar reactions to a dog's whimpering or angry barking. From that, they extrapolated that dogs and humans process emotional information in a similar way.

Poor hearing in dogs is more common in some breeds than others (Dalmatians are particularly susceptible) but, as with blindness, it's not the end of the world if your dog is deaf, especially if you're good with your hands.

There's all sorts of evidence to suggest that humans learn better if they're taught with a verbal and visual lesson simultaneously, and it's the same with dogs. That's why whenever you see people training puppies to sit, they'll do that finger or hand in the air gesture, or wave their palm towards their own chest, which is something the famous TV dog trainer Barbara Woodhouse used to do back in the 1980s.

By combining verbal and visual commands, the puppy begins to learn that whenever they hear a sound they don't really understand yet, they also see the human do whatever it is they do with their hands. And whenever those two things happen and they put their bum on the floor, for example, they get a treat. As time goes on, you'll likely drop the hand signals, but you should keep them in your locker for when you really need to emphasise something, for example when you're next to a busy road and you really need them to sit. In effect, you're telling your dog twice.

But another good reason to marry verbal and visual commands is because your dog might go deaf when they're older, like our thirteen-year-old boxer Scooby. He's been as deaf as a post for a couple of years, although he pretended to be deaf when it suited him for the previous decade!

Maybe you've got a deaf dog who likes to play rough, but is no longer able to hear your verbal commands, or indeed the other dogs' barks and squeals. If that dog is not looking in your direction, which he's unlikely to be if he's rolling around on the floor with other dogs, you've lost your principal method of communication. But if he's on a lead or a long line, you can introduce a bit of touch.

Just like verbal and hand signals, touch signals, administered through a lead or a line, must be distinct and consistent. For example, if your dog is rubbing a few other dogs up the wrong way, you can go tug-tug-tug (nothing hard, you're not trying to hurt him) and appear at his side, with a face like thunder. Actually, you can stand slightly behind him: because of that superior peripheral vision I was talking about earlier, he'll still be able to see you. Wait for him to be gentle and then give him a long, smooth stroke. He'll soon realise that being gentle with other dogs gets him what he wants.

Even dogs who weren't taught hand signals from a young age can learn them much later in life. I recently read about a Staffordshire bull terrier called Rocco who contracted an ear infection in a rescue centre in Swansea and went deaf. Rocco was eight, but RSPCA staff spent a few months teaching him the fundamentals, such as 'sit' and 'stay' and whether he'd been a good boy or not. Good for them!

Is my dog scared?

Fear in dogs manifests in different ways, but there are four main signs: fight, flight, freezing and fawning.

Most fearful dogs *look* fearful. They back off, hide behind their owner's legs, and run off given half the chance. That's flight mode, and you often hear about dogs being spooked in the park and running all the way home.

However, as with humans, fear in dogs can present as aggression. That means the hackles on a dog's back going up, his tail frantically wagging (people think that means a dog is happy, but it just means he's excited, and not necessarily in a good way), and the dog barking and lunging at people, other dogs and inanimate objects. In other words, he's gone into fight mode.

One owner described to me the day a 'switch flicked' in her Chihuahua's head, when she felt threatened by a bigger dog and decided to stand up for herself, instead of running away. The bigger dog wandered off, so the Chihuahua thought, 'Aha, that worked. From now on, I'll kick off every time anything comes near me.' (I should add that dogs don't really process size in the same way as humans, as anyone who has seen a German shepherd submit to a Jack Russell will attest.)

Owners who are embarrassed by the behaviour of their scared dogs will often become anxious and try to drag their dog away in a hurry, but the more you do that, the worse it will tend to get, because your dog will be looking at you and thinking, 'Blimey, he's in a bit of a state – now I'm even more scared!'

In human terms, think what it's like when you're on a plane going through a storm and the people either side of you are clinging on to the seats in front and looking petrified – chances are, that's going to rub off on you. But if those two people look like they don't have a worry in the world, you're more likely to feel calm. Fear is contagious. The single best thing you can do to help your dog feel safe is to act as if there isn't a problem.

If you're not a naturally ebullient and confident person, the best thing you can do for your dog is to pretend a bit – fake it till you make it – because you can't expect your dog to take the initiative.

I'll let you into a little secret: sometimes when you're watching me on the telly and everything seems fine and dandy, I'm actually thinking, 'I'm in a bit of trouble here.' So when you're walking your dog, be like me if you can: have a sunny demeanour – 'Well, isn't this lovely, darling. Hip-hip hooray!' – because it's likely that will make your dog think, 'Oh good, the boss seems fine, so everything must be OK.' After a while, you won't be pretending, you'll really be confident, because your dog will seem more at ease.

Another thing owners of scared dogs do is walk them when nobody is about, either at midnight or five in the morning. It's understandable, but what they really need to do is get them to face their fears. That doesn't mean picking your Chihuahua up and sticking it in a mad dog's face – that's a recipe for disaster – it means working out the optimum distance they can be from whatever it is they're scared of without kicking off. What you want is for them to notice whatever it is they are scared of and *not* react (and you'll want to reward that choice). Take your time. There are no prizes for rushing in this game.

Some people describe their dog as simmering before boiling over, in that their dog will start by staring and growling, with its body forward and ears back. The owner will sense that something bad is about to happen (maybe while hearing the *Jaws* music in their head), and the trick is to react early enough, before the staring and growling spills over into barking and lunging.

A good analogy is a pan of milk simmering on the stove: you take your eye off it for a moment, and when you look back, it's rising in the pan. If you grab it quickly enough and take it off the heat, it will simmer back down. But if you wait too long, it will spill over the sides and make a right mess of your cooker.

Take your dog as close as you can to another dog (or human, or skateboard, or whatever) – maybe he will be right on the cusp, clearly unhappy but not actually barking – and tell him, firmly and bluntly, 'No'. But if your dog starts looking a bit more confident and inquisitive – edging forwards, sniffing – give him a bit of praise. And if you get a good experience, quit while you're ahead, because otherwise the whole enterprise might come crashing down and you'll be back to square one. Over time, he'll be able to get closer and closer to his nemesis, until the wonderful day it ceases to be a problem.

The number one mistake people make is trying to reassure a scared dog, because the subtleties will be lost on the dog. If your dog is cowering or growling and barking, you don't want to be saying, 'It's OK. Good boy, good boy,' because your dog will be thinking, 'Oh, he thinks I'm being a good boy. WOOF! WOOF! WOOF!' Not that you want to be giving him a stern talking-to, either. Instead, it's about rewarding him with praise when he starts to look a bit more assured and inquisitive: 'Oh, good boy. Aren't you brave?'

Some dogs will freeze before going into fight mode – I once saw a Dobermann lock up and stare at another dog for three or four seconds before going berserk – while other dogs will demonstrate their fear by fawning. And that's not just a puppy thing. I worked with a Newfoundland once, a 175lb (80kg) goliath, and whenever he was afraid of another dog, which was quite often, he would throw himself on the ground and turn upside down. People think that's a sign the dog is being polite or cute, but the dog is really saying, 'Please don't hurt me . . .'.

Of course, some dogs are so scared that they don't even want to leave the house. In that case, the first question you need to ask yourself is, 'Why?' It could be a physical problem of which you're not aware, so you probably want to get her checked out at the vet. Dogs are pretty good at hiding pain, because back in the day, if their wild ancestors showed any sign of weakness, they'd get finished off. If it's not a physical problem, think what might have spooked her in the past. Either way, it's not to be ignored.

Think whether your dog has ever encountered a backfiring car or a noisy motorbike. Did someone throw their skateboard down right next to her? Did an angry dog lunge at her? And did you react in the wrong way? If you make a big deal of a poten- tially scary situation, your dog is inclined to think, 'Yeah, I thought that was scary, and the boss has just confirmed it.'

You can compare it to a parent's reaction when their tod- dler topples over on concrete for the first time. It's a fork in the road moment: either that parent can come over all hysterical – 'Oh my God! Oh my God! Are you OK, darling? Have you hurt yourself? I'm so sorry!' – or you can say, 'Never mind, it's not the end of the world. Be a brave little soldier, let's dust you down.'

If you have a dog who's afraid of the outside world and puts the emergency brake on at the front door, one of my favourite tricks is to pop her in the car (assuming you've got one), drive just a couple of streets away and park up. She'll probably be able to smell where home is, believe it or not, so she'll prob-ably lead you straight back. In doing this, you're walking her from the scary world back to safety, instead of from safety into the scary world.

It might take time, but by getting used to walking in the street, your dog will eventually pass through the front door with a hop and a skip, thinking, 'Yeah, the outside world is OK.'

Some dog phobias can sound quite comical but, as with any dog issues, they can have a profound effect on the owner.

I once worked with a lady from Birmingham who had a Great Dane called Titan. You might have seen those advertising flags they have in petrol station forecourts, the ones that look a bit like a yacht sail and flutter in the wind. Well, this lady's walk-ing route involved passing a shop with two of those sails out on the pavement. And their fluttering scared the living daylights out of poor old Titan.

He was a nervous dog at the best of times, but these weird advertising sails were his kryptonite. The week before the lady called me, Titan had seen these sails, taken flight and dragged her into the main road, right into the path of a double-decker bus, which only just stopped in time. That must have been ter-rifying for the bus driver and passengers, as well as the lady. As for Titan, it proved that he was right to have been scared of the sails, because bad things happened when he saw them.

Because the shop was only a few doors down from her house, it was almost impossible for her to avoid, which made this an almighty Great Dane-sized problem. And in order to fix things, we had to somehow convince Titan what we knew – that the sails were just sails, and they wouldn't hurt him.

Starting by walking Titan straight past the sails would have been a bad idea – I could have found myself under that very same double-decker – so we kicked off on the other side of the road instead. He could still see the sails, but they were far enough away that he didn't react. And because he didn't react, we rewarded him. Essentially, we had created a diluted version of the problem, which is often a good place to start when the problem is fear-based.

Once Titan was paying no attention at all to the sails, we crossed back over the road, but a few houses down from the shop. We walked a little loop that took us nearer and then further away from the shop, and every time he looked at the sails and didn't react, we rewarded him and told him what a good boy he was. Within an hour, we'd walk straight past the sails and he'd completely ignore them.

Not only had Titan learnt that there was nothing to worry about, sail-wise, but he'd also learnt that if he didn't pay them any attention, he'd get a treat and be told he was a good boy. I'm pleased to report that all of the lady's walks with Titan have been plain sailing ever since (sorry, I couldn't resist!).

Another rare phobia is fear of the wind, although I have come across it a couple of times. I once met a German shepherd who wouldn't leave the house if there was even a breath of wind. It didn't help that the garden was full of trees, which have a scary habit of moving around and waving their 'arms' at you a lot when it's breezy.

This dog's owner was a cigarette smoker, and whenever she had a cigarette she'd open the back door and say to the dog, 'Out you go.' But she wouldn't go out herself if the weather wasn't so nice; she'd carry on leaning against the doorframe. And the dog was translating that body language as, 'Yeah, I know it's scary out there, I wouldn't if I were you.'

I put a lead on the dog and walked around the garden, a bit further each time. And the reason she was OK doing it was because of my calm and confident demeanour – 'Hey, this is fine!' After a while, she was quite happy off the lead, especially when I started chucking a ball about. The moral of that story is, sometimes what you say with your voice is only part of the story. When it comes to dogs, actions often speak louder than words. And if you're not looking confident, you can't expect your dog to be feeling it, eh?

Is my dog fit enough?

During the Covid pandemic, Germany proposed new animal welfare laws, one of which hit the headlines: having taken advice from some expert, the German government wanted every dog to take two walks a day, totalling an hour.

Now, there will be people reading this and thinking, 'I don't see any problem with that, dogs shouldn't be cooped up in the house all day.' But that German proposal would have made some owners panic, especially those with dogs who seemed quite happy to toddle around the block, do their business and sleep for the rest of the day.

The truth is, every dog is different, so you can't have a one-size-fits-all exercise rule. If you've got a Border collie, which was bred to chase sheep for hours on end, an hour a day probably won't be enough, and he'll be climbing walls. But if you've got a ten-year-old pug and it's 30-odd degrees outside, even taking her outside for a minute would be wrong, maybe even cruel.

It's often a case of trial and error, because you might have a one-year-old Border collie who's a bit of a lazy type – and there's nothing wrong with that – or a really active seven-year-old Labrador who's as bouncy and lean as you like. You'll just know from their behaviour if you're getting their exercise regime right or not. And if they're happy and relaxed, you probably are too.

If you're not getting it right, it can cause all sorts of problems, because exercise doesn't just improve physical wellbeing, it also improves mental wellbeing. That's why sticking your dog in the back garden, however big it is, is no substitute for a proper walk, because they need to be out there experiencing the wider world. Every time a dog sniffs a lamppost, that's like them reading the local newspaper, finding out what's been going on in their manor.

I actually split my dog walks into two modes: what I call 'on duty' walking, which is when I lead the way, we walk at my pace and I decide when to stop; and what I call 'break time', which is when I let them go off and do their own thing. They can lead me wherever, sniff whatever they like and say hello to other dogs. It's all fascinating stuff for a dog and stimulates their mind.

During Covid lockdown, lots of people got a taste of what it feels like being confined to a house on their own for days on end. That isolation and lack of interaction caused lots of mental health issues, and it's the same for dogs. And when you've got an anxious, hyperactive dog, it can be a bit of a nightmare, and often leads to the dog being walked even less. It's not hard to see how that can become a downward spiral.

One family I worked with, the dog went out the front door, got very excited and started barking. Halfway through the consultation, I asked if it happened every time, and the dad replied, 'Well, every time we do take him out . . . ' It turned out they were only walking the dog a couple of times a week, because they were so embarrassed by his behaviour. But that had created a catch-22 situation, whereby he was getting more and more excited at the prospect of a walk, and his behaviour was getting more and more extreme.

It is possible for a dog to do too much exercise. You have to be very careful with puppies, because their young joints can be damaged, which causes lots of problems in later life. Otherwise, it very much depends on the breed and age of your dog. A rule of thumb for the first year or so of your dog's life is: 'five minutes' walk for every month of life'. So, a five-month-old puppy should not exceed 25 minutes of walking (5 x 5). I've lost count of the number of owners I've heard walking small puppies for an hour or more, blissfully unaware. It's important to note that all puppies and dogs are different, so have a chat with your vet about yours.

I once worked with a dog whose hyperactivity had got so bad, the whole family were walking him in shifts, amounting to at least four hours a day. In the end, they created a super-fit athlete of a dog. But when I asked if all that exercise had made him any less hyperactive, the answer was, 'Not really. In fact it's getting worse.' That's when it twigged that they'd created a dog with loads of stamina who could effortlessly keep up his bad behaviour for hours on end. Lack of exercise hadn't been the root cause of the problem in the first place and so more exercise was never likely to be the solution.

I always say to people, 'If you're thinking about getting a dog, be sure to match the breed to your own lifestyle.' So, if you're an avid runner, get a dog that likes to run (but maybe not a greyhound or a whippet, because while they like to run, they don't run for very long – they go like the clappers for a couple of minutes and spend the rest of the day sleeping!). And if you're quite a sedentary soul, get a plodder.

I often come across dogs that aren't getting enough exercise – and it causes all sort of problems. Herding and working breeds, such as Border collies, spaniels and cattle dogs, are most likely to be affected. Spending too long in a 'comfortable' environment in a house can drive them stir-crazy, so it's really important to get those kinds of breeds out and about for long-ish periods.

I'm often asked, 'What's the right amount of exercise?' But there's no single answer; it varies from breed to breed and from dog to dog. At the same time, lots of problems, such as disruptive and overexcitable behaviour, can be improved, if not cured, simply by making sure your dog gets enough exercise.

I'm sometimes asked if a dog can be overtrained, usually because the owner is afraid their pooch is going to turn into some kind of half-dog, half-robot. I wouldn't say a dog can be *over*trained, but I would say they can be trained in such a way that drains their spirit. And none of us want that.

The old-fashioned way of training was largely based on punishment and could be quite brutal. Dogs who underwent that kind of training were sometimes obedient, but they were also scared and downbeat, as if they'd been broken. That's very different to modern training methods, which are about training dogs to be in control and well mannered, without snuffing out their personality. Because, let's face it, we all love dogs to be a bit mischievous and cheeky.

As for people who enter their dogs into competitions – stuff like doggy agility and heelwork to music, which require intensive training – a lot of dogs love it. I'm sure there are competitive dog parents who are driven more by the trophies and rosettes they can stick on the mantelpiece than their dog's enjoyment, but most people are in it for the right reasons.

Is my dog unwell or in pain?

As I've already touched on, dogs are very good at concealing pain, but there are still telltale signs.

A dog in pain might not want to jump off the sofa or out of the car, which would suggest they've got a problem with their front paws. They might be sensitive to the touch (the classic is when you try to touch their paw and they wince, yelp or pull it away). Or your normally friendly, cuddly pooch might suddenly start baring their teeth and/or growling if you go anywhere near them.

Signs of sickness are usually more subtle. Your dog might be withdrawn and less playful than normal. You'll throw him a ball and he'll just look at it forlornly, rather than bounding after it. He might not want to eat. One of my dogs is quite picky so it's not unusual for him to turn his nose up at a treat, but another one would normally eat a scabby horse, so I know that if I offer him a treat and he doesn't want it, there's something seriously amiss.

It all comes down to knowing your dog – but there's only so much they can communicate. It's not as though they can sidle up to you on the sofa and say, 'Sorry I'm not as playful as usual, but I've got a splitting headache.' I often wonder if dogs can just get out of bed the wrong side sometimes. We accept that humans have off days every now and again, so maybe dogs have them, too.

There are no real-life Doctor Dolittles, so mostly owners and vets surmise what might be going on by observing the dog's reactions. So, if you see a vet checking an older dog for mobility, they'll bring the back leg up and watch carefully to see what they do. If the dog winces, makes a sound or maybe their ears flatten back, it's not unreasonable to assume they are saying, 'Crikey, that hurt!'

Is my dog too excited?

Is there such a thing as a dog that's too excited? Surely everyone wants a dog who's friendly and happy to see people. Well, not if their version of excitement is jumping all over their family and everything else, all day and every day.

In the English-speaking world, people tend to think that happy dogs are excited dogs. But as I've discussed elsewhere in this book, there are lots of different types of excitement, not just happy excitement.

When people are asked to describe a happy dog, they never say 'a dog peacefully dozing in front of the fire'. But lots of dogs are happy and calm. That's why nobody has ever phoned me up and said, 'Graeme, come quickly, my dog's too calm!' and why you can never over-praise a dog for his calmness. It's when a dog gets revved up that problems happen, whether it's aggression, separation anxiety, barking at traffic or stealing food.

In the very early days of my dog training business, I met a guy with a three-year-old boxer called Buster. Boxers are affectionately known by their owners as the jokers of the dog world, which I've always known to be true (our boxer still makes us laugh, even though he's getting on a bit). And Buster was very keen to show anyone who came near that he was typical of his breed.

This wasn't a problem for most people, except for Dad. He explained to me: 'Any time I come in from work, Buster jumps all over me. He doesn't do it with anyone else and I can't tell you how many suits he's ruined. I try my best to fend him off, shout at him, ask him to sit down, try giving him treats. But the more I try to stop him from jumping all over me, the worse he gets.'

Then this guy said something really important: 'The weird thing is, he doesn't do it on the weekend, only in the week.' I thought, 'Hang on a minute, Buster knows the days of the week?!' Then the guy explained that he only ever wears jeans and a T-shirt on the weekend, which is when the penny dropped.

As soon as Buster heard the sound of his owner's BMW pulling up on the driveway, he knew what would happen next – Dad would appear wearing his suit, and if Buster jumped up at him, Dad would get agitated. And the more Buster jumped, the more Dad would fling his arms around and push him back, which is the greatest game known to dog. In other words, Buster had come to equate his dad wearing a suit with quality play time. On the other hand, if he jumped up at Dad while he was wearing jeans and a T-shirt, he'd barely react. And because no one else he met wore a 'play suit', he didn't jump up at them either.

An adult boxer jumping at a fully grown man is one thing, but dogs being excited around children is quite another. That's why lots of parents want to know if it's possible to keep a dog calm while their kids carry on playing.

It goes without saying that young children can be very energetic themselves, and it isn't really an option to involve the youngest ones in training. So the first thing I'd suggest is teaching your dog the difference between his toys and the kids' toys.

To do this, put your kids' toys on one side of the room and your dog's toys on the other side. While he's on his lead, take him towards his toys and if he picks one up, tell him what a good boy he is, so he's associating praise with the sight and smell of his toys. Then lead him to the kids' toys, and if he looks like he's going to pick one up, firmly but calmly tell him no and, if need be, stand between him and the toys. Repeat this process, until he's no longer picking up any of the kids' toys and, as time goes on, bring the two groups of toys closer together, and maybe even start mixing them up.

When you're confident your dog has cracked it, you can reintroduce the kids. And if it gets too much again, tell him no, remove him from the situation, and reintroduce him when he, and the kids, have calmed down.

Most dog owners will know what I mean by a dog having the 'zoomies', which is that time of the day when they go absolutely crazy and run all over the house. It often happens as soon as their owner starts to get ready to take them for a walk, and it can sometimes spill over into a habit so that it occurs every time you leave the house.

It's easy to inadvertently reward dogs in that situation. I once worked with a French bulldog who wouldn't let any of his family members out of the house without a ruckus. He'd jump up and nip, and the whole situation had been super-charged by some wonky advice to throw treats in the corner of the room before opening the door and making a run for it. During the consultation, he tried to grab a treat and instead bit his mum's finger as she was about to throw them. The problem was that throwing treats one way and running the other had created an exciting competition. And excitement was the very last thing they needed!

I recommend forensically analysing your pre-leaving the house routine. What do you do or say when you get off the sofa? What about when you pick up the car keys? Or when you put your coat on? The trigger for a dog's excitement can start even before you stand up to depart.

Many years ago, I lived with a Jack Russell who would bark and whine every time I went to leave the house. I eventually realised that he was reacting to me saying, 'Right, then!' before I hauled my backside off the sofa!

It might sound like a lot of rigmarole, but once you've broken your pre-leaving the house routine down, you can reward them, or not, at every stage. So reward them for not kicking off when you stand up. If they do kick off, tell them no, reward them for quietening down, and repeat the process. It might take a couple of hours of practice, but eventually you'll be able to get through the door without your dog going loopy. Take your time. It's not a race.

Some dogs come across as bossy, another form of over-excitement. Someone once contacted me about their cockapoo who'd go berserk every time their family was out for a walk and one or more of them would enter a shop. Then when the family members came out again, this cockapoo would react like she hadn't seen them in years. She'd also go nuts if they were at the beach and the pack separated. In effect, she was saying, 'Oi! What do you think you're doing? Come back here!' In that case, it was about teaching the dog that it wasn't the barking that brought people back, and teaching his family that there should be negative consequences for her barking (they didn't walk straight back to her) and praise for when she didn't.

Is my dog lazy?

Owners often worry that their dogs are sleeping too much, probably because we humans associate lying around for long periods with being unwell, either physically or mentally.

But a dog sleeping for 14 or 15 hours a day is quite normal. And if it's hot, they might sleep for even more than 15 hours – and who can blame them? I should add that it's also not unusual for puppies to sleep 18 hours a day.

All dogs have different sleeping schedules, depending on age, size, the amount of exercise they do and air temperature. But in terms of their nighttime sleep, they'll usually have a similar pattern to humans. In our house, that's roughly 11pm to 7am. During the day, most dogs will take naps every now and again, but just because their eyes are closed doesn't necessarily mean they're in a deep slumber. They might just be resting or dozing, ready to leap out of bed at the sound of a bag of treats being shaken.

As long as your dog seems bright-eyed and bushy-tailed when she is awake, there's no need to worry. However, any sudden changes in sleep pattern might be cause for concern. For example, there might be something amiss if you put your dog's food bowl down and she stays resolutely in her bed, because most dogs will emerge like a food-seeking missile. You know your dog better than anyone. If you struggle to rouse your dog from a particularly long sleep, you should take her to a vet.

I do hear of people who are worried about their dog sleeping too much dragging them out of bed, making them play and taking them for loads of walks. But if you do that, you can end up with a hyperactive dog who never settles. I think what often happens is that owners feel guilty that their dog must be sleeping all the time because they're bored and need entertaining when in fact she's just being a dog, quite happily dreaming about being entertained.

If you've ever been to a country where there are lots of stray dogs on the streets, you'll have noticed that they spend most of their time lying in the shade, conserving energy. If they are up and about, they'll often be looking for food. And while they're on a mission and can travel considerable distances, they certainly won't be running anywhere. They'll be covering ground at an efficient, steady pace.

That's how dogs behave when they're not under human supervision. Naturally, that's not the same as saying you should keep your dog locked away in the house all day and tell yourself he's happy (but then . . . you bought this book, so you're not that kind of person, right?). The fact is, those strays might sleep a lot, but they'll be getting plenty of mental stimulation through hunting for scraps.

Is my dog an optimist?

When I was filming in Australia, what struck me was that while the dogs were pretty much the same as British dogs (perhaps they bark with a different accent), the owners were generally more optimistic that I'd be able to fix their problem. 'I'll give it a go!' was a phrase I heard a lot in Australia.

We do optimism in the UK too, of course, but just occasionally I get owners saying things like, 'Yeah, by all means try to fix my dog, but I doubt it's going to work.' For example, I went to see one guy who'd moved with his little dog from Manchester to the Lake District (presumably Manchester wasn't rainy enough for him). This little lad was really reactive, and he would snarl and bark at everyone and everything. But after three or four hours of my training, he was walking around the village as calm as anything. When we got back to their house, the owner said to me, 'You know what? I really didn't think you'd be able to do anything.' I thought, 'What kind of mentality is that? It's just so British.' This guy had essentially bet good money that he'd be wasting it, because his would be the one dog I wouldn't be able to fix! Maybe it's the rain . . .

There has been quite a bit of research into whether some dogs are more optimistic than others – or, as the scientists would put it, whether dogs demonstrate 'cognitive bias', which is the tendency to act in an irrational way because of our limited ability to process information objectively.

Back in 2010, the University of Bristol published a study that categorised dogs as optimistic or pessimistic. They also found that dogs who were generally calm when left alone by their owners were more likely to have a 'bowl half full' outlook on life, while those who suffered from separation anxiety were more likely to have a 'bowl half empty' mentality.

In the first half of the study, every dog was taken into a room and trained to walk over to a bowl that was full of food when placed at one end of the room and empty when placed at the other. When the dogs had worked out the difference, the scientists moved the bowls to the middle of the room and observed how quickly each dog went to the bowl. Sure enough, the most anxious dogs were slowest to approach the bowls in the middle of the room (you can imagine them thinking, 'Of course there's no food in those bowls. What's the point, life's rubbish, there'll never be any food ever again), while the less anxious dogs couldn't get to those bowls quick enough, suggesting they were more optimistic.

You might reasonably be thinking, 'Maybe the dogs who were slow to approach the bowls were just a bit daft' – which is a fair point – but I quite like that dogs might be classed as optimistic or pessimistic. Many certainly seem that way: the optimist, always hopeful that their owner will have a treat handy, or the pessimist, always looking at you as if to say, 'Nah, she'll have nothing for me today ...'

How do dogs find their way home?

There are competing theories as to how dogs can find their way home – and none of them involve GPS. Actually, at least one of them does . . .

One of the more recent studies, published by the Czech University of Life Sciences and Virginia Tech in 2020, tracked the navigational abilities of 27 dogs over three years and more than 600 trials. The dogs were walked through a forest by their owners, off the lead, until they scented prey and legged it. After a certain amount of time, the owners called their dogs back, and the dogs had to find their way back to them.

About 60 per cent of the dogs followed their outbound track home. Sensible. I mean, that's what you or I might do. But in a third of cases, the dogs ran back and forth along the north-south axis before making their way home along a different route. And those dogs found their owners quicker than those that used their noses. From that information, the researchers extrapolated that those initial 'compass runs' helped the dogs orient themselves. Intriguing, isn't it?

We already suspected that lots of creatures have what you might call a 'magnetic sense', which they use for navigation. Pigeons and migratory birds are the obvious examples, but turtles, amphibians, insects and some mammals are also thought to use magnetic-based navigation – although some scientists think there are other things involved, including smell, sound and the sun.

I suspect that in most cases, when dogs are lost not far from home, they rely primarily on their noses. So there's probably a lot of sniffing the air and thinking, 'Hang on a minute, that smells like the fish and chip shop on the corner, I'll head in that direction.' By stringing those olfactory clues – or landmarks – together, eventually they'll find their way home, although sight probably kicks in the closer they get – 'I know this bridge, almost there . . .'

There are some incredible stories about lost dogs making epic journeys home. In 2012, a guy from South Carolina dropped off his Labrador Bucky at his dad's place in Virginia, because he wasn't allowed dogs in his apartment. Eight months later, Bucky was found in a forest back in South Carolina. When the chap who found Bucky took him to the vet, his microchip revealed who he belonged to. Bucky had travelled 500 miles, and I imagine the reunion was wonderful to see.

On a personal note, I once visited someone who had just moved to Swindon. On the very first day, they waved goodbye to the removal men, had their first cup of tea in their new home, and then took the dog for a walk. He'd only been off the lead a few minutes when he bolted across a field and over the horizon. Horrified, everyone in the family turned out looking for the dog for two hours, to no avail. But when they got home, there he was, sitting on the doorstep, with a look that said, 'What took you so long?' That can only be the power of smell.

There's also the tale of my dad's German shepherd, which he had during the Second World War, when everybody called them Alsatians (for some reason, there was a certain sensitivity about the label 'German' at the time . . .). One day, his dad (my granddad) decided this dog had to go, for reasons lost in the mists of time, so he was ferried from Selby, where they lived, to Garforth, near Leeds, which is 15 miles away. Two weeks later, the dog turned up on their doorstep. When my dad told me that story when I was a cynical teenager, I thought, 'Yeah, of course he did, Dad ...' But now, I'm sure he was telling the truth. The fact is that even now, decades later, there's a lot we still don't understand about how dogs do some of the things they do.

Are dogs sun worshippers?

Temperature is a funny thing when it comes to dogs. The basic rule of thumb is that when it gets really hot – as in the mercury is touching 30 degrees – don't take your dog for a walk. However, it is very much horses for courses.

Brachycephalic breeds (bulldogs, pugs, Boston terriers, boxers, anything with a flattened nose) don't pant so effectively and can't drag as much air in as long-nosed dogs, which means they're prone to heatstroke and heat exhaustion. It doesn't matter if they grew up in Dubai or Derby, taking them out when the sun's blazing is not a good idea.

People talk about their brachycephalic dog's breathing sounding like it's out of control, and if it's going nineteen to the dozen, it probably is getting that way. But all dogs need exercise, so the best thing to do is walk your pug or French bulldog when it's a bit cooler, either early in the morning or late at night.

Many years ago, I attended a convention in Germany, where there were dog trainers from all over Europe. I got chatting to some guys from Seville who were training dogs for competitions, and my first question was, 'How on earth do you do two or three hours of training a day in the summer Seville heat?' They explained that they trained at five o'clock in the morning and under floodlights in the late evening. That's an extreme example, but the same principle applies.

Humans sweat all over their bodies, and when the sweat evaporates it cools us down, but dogs only sweat from the pads on their paws, which is not an efficient cooling technique. Instead, they pant, which involves breathing in air, humidifying it, and then exhaling it, which increases the evaporation from their noses and lungs (think of a dog's tongue as a car radiator). That's why dogs pant a lot more when it's hot, and the further their tongue is hanging out of their mouths, the more over-heated they're likely to be.

But panting is a pretty rubbish cooling system as well (despite the fact that many mammals, most birds and some reptiles do it), which is why, even for non-brachycephalic breeds, a 30-minute walk in 30-degree heat is not recommended, at least in the UK.

However, if you live in a country where 30-degree heat is normal, you'll probably find that dogs can acclimatise, like humans. That's why when you go to hot countries, you'll see people happily playing with their dogs over the park after work when it's still 30-plus degrees.

I was quite surprised to see lots of Rottweilers in Australia, because my two, Axel and Gordon, used to struggle in the heat. Rotties aren't brachycephalic, but some of them do have two coats of dark fur, which you'd think would absorb heat. It does, and of course there are limits, but they undoubtedly cope better than our dogs in that kind of heat.

Something else to think about is the surface temperature of pavements and roads. It doesn't really matter where in the world you are, here's the golden rule: if it's too hot to put your hand on it for, let's say, five seconds, it's too hot to walk your dog on it. In the UK, it's usually just a case of waiting for the next cloud to come over, although protective booties are *de rigueur* in places where temperatures regularly hit 40 degrees and tarmac can be hotter than the centre of the sun.

Some people put sunscreen on their dogs, which isn't as mad as it sounds. If your dog has light-coloured, thin fur – think a white English bull terrier with pink skin showing on his nose – there's no reason why you wouldn't slap a bit of factor 50 on him, because why would you want a dog with a suntan anyway? (Saying that, there's probably a grooming parlour somewhere in California that gives dogs spray tans.)

At the other end of the spectrum, some dogs obviously feel the cold more than others, which begs the question: should your dog ever wear clothes?

I sometimes see dogs strolling around in woolly jumpers in the summer, which obviously isn't right. If you're dressing your dog up when it's warm, you're likely doing it out of vanity – your vanity, not the dog's. Here's some simple advice: don't.

Most dogs, especially breeds that originated in chillier parts of the world, don't need to wear anything, however cold it is. They have a saying in places where they do mushing: you know how cold the night is by the number of huskies you need in your tent. I have it on good authority that a three-dog night is a very cold night indeed. But left to their own devices, huskies are quite happy to bed down in the snow, which is why you'll never see a husky in an anorak. Quite apart from the fact they're just too stylish. Obvs.

However, some dogs lack a natural defence against the cold – an extreme example would be a hairless Chinese crested dog – so if it's a bit chilly outside, it might be a good idea to get them togged up before leaving the warmth of your home. And if it's very cold, you might need extra measures. I'm told that in Canada, some dogs wear rubber booties, or have Vaseline applied to their paws, to protect against a painful build-up of compacted snow and ice between their toes. Your dog might not get frostbite if you don't put a coat on him, as sometimes happens in particularly cold countries, but he could get hypothermia. Warning signs include shivering, lethargy and whining.

Smaller dogs (Chihuahuas), slimmer dogs (whippets), short-haired dogs (greyhounds) and less active dogs (pugs) can all benefit from an extra layer, while age can also be a factor, as it is for our boxer: he went years without wearing anything other than a happy face, but started shivering when he hit 12, so I went out and bought him a fetching racing green fleece (that's the other thing about clothes on dogs, they just make people smile). I stopped short of getting him a cravat because that would be ridiculous. Who wears a cravat any more?!

Clothing aside, the best advice for particularly cold conditions is simply to shorten your usual walking route and keep your dog moving, or not take them out at all if it means ploughing through drifts of snow. Also, make sure you dry your dog thoroughly when you get home, paying special attention to their paws if the roads have been gritted. Toxins in antifreeze and sodium chloride in rock salt can cause irritation, while grit and sharp ice can cause lacerations.

Can dogs and cats get on?

There's no way of knowing for certain whether dogs know that humans aren't dogs, but we can be confident they do.

First, we're not particularly hairy and stand on two legs. Second, dogs have incredible noses, and humans don't smell like dogs. Third, studies have shown that dogs are naturally more sociable with humans than they are with other dogs (how lucky are we, right?). We're also fairly certain that dogs know cats aren't one of their clan – and cats look and act a lot more like dogs than humans do.

I often hear stories about boy meeting girl and their dogs not getting on, but when boy meets girl, boy has dog and girl has cat (or the other way around), it can be even trickier.

I've visited plenty of houses where dogs and cats rub along quite happily, thank you very much. They're usually fed in different areas and sleep in different beds, but I've also seen lots of cases of dogs and cats eating together nicely before snuggling up next to each other on the sofa.

But most anecdotal evidence from owners suggests that most dog–cat relationships are based on tolerance, and nothing more. A 2018 study by the University of Lincoln, involving a survey of 748 mixed-species homes, revealed that most owners believed their dog and cat got along 'amicably', which was defined as 'a friendly, mutual bond, which is recognisable through the use of affiliative behaviours, maintaining proximity and effective, non-aggressive communication between individuals'. Nice. However, not all owners categorised the relationship between their dog and their cat as close.

It was also found that cats were more likely to threaten dogs than vice versa (instances of dogs threatening cats were rare); they hardly ever shared food, toys or beds; and they almost never groomed each other. All in all, it's not exactly one of the great love stories, is it?

As to why cats seem to have more beef with dogs than the other way around, the study's authors speculated it was because cats are at an earlier stage of domestication than dogs, physiologically and behaviourally. But the main takeaway from the study is how little we really know about dog–cat relationships. Owner surveys have their limitations, because questions are open to interpretation – one owner's comfortable dog or cat might be another owner's nervous dog or cat, because they're reading the signs differently, or not reading them at all.

A 2020 Italian survey found that while dogs and cats have different body language, they can understand each other and respond accordingly, much like two humans who can't speak each other's lingo. For example, if a cat approaches a dog with its tail up, the dog will react in a friendly manner; but if the dog approaches a cat with its tail up, the cat will react aggressively.

Whenever someone asks if I can train a dog to become buddies with a cat, I always need to know about the cat's temperament first.

If the cat stands its ground when confronted with a dog (i.e. arches its back and hisses), they will often come to a peaceful agreement, especially if the dog is calm or submissive (I've seen some hilarious situations where a big, powerful dog has been more than a little bit wary of a pussycat). But if the cat is scaredy and prone to running and the dog is hyperactive, it's likely to be an uphill struggle, and can end up in disaster.

Preferably, you'd rear a dog and a cat together, or at least introduce a dog when the cat is still very young. If you've had a cat for a while, and you're thinking about getting a rescue dog, get one who has lived with cats before without any problems. Indoor cats have been shown to be more tolerant towards dogs than outdoor cats, and maybe avoid getting a hunting dog, because it's very difficult to stop them following their chasing instinct ('prey drive'), or a sheepdog, because cats don't really like being herded.

Trying to force a dog and a cat to be best buddies, because you think them sleeping in the same bed will look cute, is probably not going to work. For example, putting a cat in a crate, plonking it in the middle of the living room and letting your dog sniff around it is just going to terrify the cat. You have to let them come to their own accommodation in their own time.

I've seen some amazing cat–dog workarounds. A few years ago, I visited a house in the Black Country that had what looked like giant, cartoon mouse holes in the walls, but at ceiling level, connected by shelves that started above the curtain pelmet and continued all the way around the rooms and even up the stairs. When I asked what these holes and shelves were for, I was told that they were for the cat, to keep her away from the dog. It wasn't an ideal scenario – you'd rather have two pets who were great chums – but it was an ingenious piece of engineering and served its purpose. The cat and dog shared the whole house, but on two different levels.

Can dogs tell the time?

It often feels as though our dogs know what time it is, and they kind of do. They'll expect to be fed at the same time every day, let out for a wee at the same time every day, walked at the same time every day. They seem to know what hour you'll be home from work, when to get up and when to go to bed.

But just because they know when things are supposed to happen, that doesn't mean they have a concept of time, at least not in the human sense.

Your dog probably distinguishes the sound of your car's engine from other people's. He knows when it's dinnertime because he's picked up on various clues that dinner is on its way: you've just arrived home from work; you're preparing your own dinner; there's however much sunlight. He knows when it's time to go for a walk because you've both finished dinner and you're changing into your jeans and sweatshirt, for example. It's just a case of habit and repetition.

However, dogs do have a circadian rhythm, which is an internal clock that tells them when it's daylight or nightfall, and therefore when they should be awake or asleep. And Dr Alexandra Horowitz, a leading researcher in dog cognition, has suggested that dogs might even be able to *smell* the time.

Horowitz's theory is that because dogs can detect both new (strong) and old (weak) scents, a dog might associate the diminishing scent of a human in the house with the passage of time. That ties in with a 2010 Swedish study that found that dogs seemed more excited to see their owners after being left alone for two hours compared to 30 minutes, while there was no noticeable difference in their reaction between a two-hour and four-hour separation.

A 2018 Northwestern University study on mice showed that previously unknown neurons within the brain's temporal lobe, where spatial memory is encoded, are triggered when they're waiting for something to happen, which is another indication that animals are able to judge a portion of time.

Each mouse scampered along a track until it reached a closed door, where the floor was a different texture. After exactly six seconds, the door opened and the mouse carried on and collected a treat. Then, after the mouse had done that a few times, the researchers got rid of the virtual door. However, when the mouse felt the textured floor under its feet, it still waited exactly six seconds before carrying on and picking up its treat.

While all this was going on, the researchers were recording what was going on in the mice's brains, and they discovered that when the mice stopped at the door, the cells that control spatial encoding went into lockdown and a new set of cells switched on. This suggests that the mice were counting down those six seconds before ploughing forwards.

Of course, mice aren't very small dogs, so we can't just assume that the same is going on in a dog's brain. That said, the results of the experiment tally with the experiences of owners and trainers: dogs can very quickly work out how long they have to wait for a reward, which is why good trainers often dole out treats at random intervals to keep dogs keen. Also, the study isn't suggesting that animals can instinctively judge the passing of time, because the mice had to learn the process.

While we're on the subject of the passing of time, you might still think that one human year is roughly equal to seven dog years, because that theory has been doing the rounds forever (that figure was apparently based on dividing a human life expectancy of 77 by a dog life expectancy of 11).

But a 2019 study by researchers from the University of San Diego suggested things were more complicated. For starters, some dogs are sexually mature by the time they're six months old (a human's three-and-a-half years according to the traditional conversion method), while the reportedly oldest dog ever – Bobi, a Rafeiro do Alentejo from Portugal – was 31. In fact, Bobi's owners claimed he was 31 years and 165 days old when he died in 2023, and by the old conversion rules he would have been almost 220 years old, nearly 100 years older than the oldest ever human. Throw in the fact that small breeds have significantly longer life expectancies than larger breeds, and straight dog–human age comparisons become ever trickier.

What is age anyway? Of course, there's chronological age, but there's also biological age, which is based on the condition your body is in, regardless of how many years you've been alive. If you've spent a lot of time eating bad food, drinking too much alcohol and smoking cigarettes, your biological age is likely to be higher than your chronological age – or you might be 50 and have the body of a 30-year-old, because you've been *so* good (and perhaps lucky, having inherited good genes).

Dog-wise, using biological age makes more sense. But if you go online in an effort to find an alternative to the simple but crude 'multiply by seven' method, there are loads of different ways to convert doggy years to human years, enough to make your head spin. Most of them take into account that dogs age far quicker than humans at first, but that then their ageing slows. The San Diego researchers, for instance, reckoned that a dog's first year is roughly equal to 31 human years, yet by the age of eight they are the equivalent of a 64-year-old human.

Anyone who's ever had a dog would already have known that the old conversion method didn't make much sense, but you might be taken aback by the idea that your still spritely six-year-old is already well into middle age. You might also be more understanding when your eight-year-old's enthusiasm for chasing a ball starts to wane, because the chances are that you won't be chasing a ball around either when you hit your mid-60s – at least not with quite the same zip as you did in your 20s!

Whichever method we choose to apply, it's clear that a dog's age is relative to his breed. A ten-year-old Great Dane would be a very elderly gent, whereas a cheeky Jack Russell born on the same day might well be described as 'middle-aged'. (Do dogs have mid-life crises? That's a question for which science has no answer . . . yet!).

With dogs having become such an integral part of human society, it's easy to forget that before they buddied up with us, they spent millions of years evolving to suit an entirely different environment. That means they experience the world in very different ways, but also that they're able to shed light on a lot of mysteries.

Who knows what secrets remain unlocked in dogs' brains? As it is, dogs can help us with everything from hunting down criminals to detecting diseases. But if we manage to find the keys to their thinking, the possibilities could be almost endless.

Chapter 5

Why Do Dogs . . . ?

Despite years of harmonious co-existence, most people still don't know why dogs do a lot of the things they do.

Dogs are like living, breathing puzzles, and even though we've got some of our brightest minds on the case, we'll probably never solve them. If only the frustrating little blighters would hurry up and learn to speak!

But as science advances, dogs become less and less mysterious – and at least nowadays we can make educated suggestions, rather than relying on our hunches (which, by the way, are often quite accurate).

So here's a rundown of some of the most asked questions by dog owners, with answers from me and some brilliant canine scientists – by which I means humans in lab coats. Dogs aren't quite that smart. Yet . . .

Why do dogs howl?

While all breeds are capable of howling, it's more prevalent in some breeds than others (beagles and huskies spring to mind), while some owners report that they've never heard their dog howl.

Howling in dogs is a throwback behaviour: wolves howl to bring the pack back together before and after hunts, just as a dog with separation anxiety is howling to bring his human or dog pack back together.

If a dog is howling in conjunction with certain sounds, the problem sometimes gets out of control – often because when they started doing it as a youngster, their owners thought it was funny and encouraged them. Ice cream vans can trigger howling, as can the *Coronation Street* theme tune. Random, I know, but a few people have told me that, and I think it must be that first soaring trumpet note that dogs mistake for howling. And if owners aren't encouraging it, they're probably telling their dogs to pack it in, which could be just as bad. (All attention is good attention to some dogs!)

There are loads of clips on the internet of dogs playing the piano and howling along (when I say they're playing the piano, I'm not talking about a Chopin concerto, I just mean they're banging their paws on the keys). If you could speak to those dogs and ask them why they were doing it, they'd probably reply, 'I dunno. That noise just makes me howl for some reason. What I do know is the humans seem to like me doing it. Smile! You're on camera . . .'

I once met a music teacher who was having great difficulty teaching music to her students at home because every time she played piano, violin or sang, the dog would join in. That might have been fine had he been able to hold a note, but he was horribly off-key.

This lady had tried giving her dog treats to shut him up, but that was just rewarding him for his bad behaviour. Instead, I decided to take a mini violin lesson, so I could at least make a noise on the violin to train the dog (I'm a far better dog trainer than I am a violinist, in case you were wondering).

Why do dogs bark?

I've got a friend who's a radio presenter, and he used to take his little dog Riley into the studio with him all the time. It didn't always go well – like the time the dog decided to be amorous with a guest's bagpipes which had been laid on the studio floor during an interview (!) – but for all his adult life, although he wasn't necessarily silent all day and every day, when he was in that studio, he just knew when to keep schtum. It was very impressive.

The reason was that, from when he was brought to the studio as a puppy, if he was quiet, especially when that red 'on air' light was on, he'd get a tickle and a titbit and this continued on and off throughout his life. The on-air light was his cue: 'When the light goes on, humans talk, but you chill out.' He was so relaxed in fact that on more than one occasion he could be heard snoring in the background of the broadcast. Delightful! The lesson being: if you want to avoid having a barky dog, don't focus on the barking, focus on the quiet bits.

We usually forget to reward dogs when they're being good, because when they're being good, they fall off our radar. They're asleep in their bed or sitting on the sofa, staring contentedly at the world outside. And if you do remember to praise your dog for their quietness, there's a chance you might sound too excited (traditionally, a lot of dog training is based on using excitement in your voice). What you need to do instead is praise them in a gentle way, as calm as you'd like them to stay: 'Good lad, very nice, well done.' In other words, 'I love it when you're quiet.' Top tip: stretch your words out. You might be surprised how much calmer you sound when it takes twice as long to say. Gooood booooooyyy . . .

Not long ago, I met a Hungarian vizsla called Xander. His owners told me he was a classic Jekyll and Hyde character – as good as gold with everyone in the family, but very different with visitors. As soon as Xander heard someone outside, he'd sprint towards the door, lunge, bark and bare his teeth. One time, he even bit a nervous family friend who tried to fend him off.

When I rocked up, Xander went nuts, but I knew I wasn't in danger. He was making an awful lot of noise, and lunging like crazy, but he was doing it from a few feet away. Every now and again, he'd back up a few inches, before rushing forwards again. This wasn't a dog that wanted to hurt me; this was a dog who was scared, stuck somewhere between fight and flight, and wanted me to go away.

We've always had nervous dogs, that's just in their DNA. But since the Covid pandemic and all those lockdowns, I've seen more and more dogs overreacting to 'stranger danger'. This sudden rise can't have anything to do with nature because evolution doesn't happen that quickly. Therefore, this behaviour must have been learnt. Or, more correctly, Xander and other dogs are behaving like that because of what they *haven't* learnt.

Xander was born in early 2020, just as the UK and the rest of the world were locking down. For months, strangers didn't enter the house, which Xander thought was perfectly normal, because he'd never known any different. But when lockdown eased, and suddenly people he'd never met before were wandering into *his* home, sitting down on *his* sofa and chatting away to members of *his* family, Xander, quite understandably, couldn't get his head around it.

What made things even more confusing was that the only people who had come to the door during lockdown were delivering things, and Xander had convinced himself that he'd made them all run away by barking. Without exception, they complied.

It's worth remembering that while a barking, lunging dog isn't necessarily being aggressive, the person they're barking at might not know that, so visitors need to be briefed before they enter the house. The headline advice to visitors is to act normal. And by normal, I mean acting as if the dog isn't even there. When they enter the house, position yourself between your dog and them, and calmly but firmly tell your dog 'No'. Don't shout or scream it, because that might rev your dog up even more or make him even more nervous.

When your dog starts backing down, reward him with quiet, soothing praise, so that the message is clear: barking and lunging aren't acceptable, but being calm is lovely. And when your dog seems content, maybe reward him with a few titbits. If you follow that advice, your dog and your mate will be thick as thieves in no time.

When I was on tour in 2022, I was joined on stage in Leeds by a Staffordshire bull terrier called Bear. Bear had ended up in Manchester Dogs' Home after being found wandering the streets as a puppy, and in 2014 he survived a fire at the facility, which killed 50 of his pals, including his kennel mate. As a result of all that trauma, Bear was a very nervous dog indeed.

If anything spooked Bear, he'd bark and bark until the spooker (is that a word?) went away. And they always did go away, because Staffies can be quite intimidating. As with Xander and the delivery people, Bear's behaviour became self-rewarding and deeply ingrained. Though of course, Xander only imagined he was scaring the intruders away: Bear actually was.

Bear's owner was at her wits' end. Ignoring his barking hadn't worked, and she felt bad telling him off, because of his horrific back story. Luckily, she didn't have to tell Bear off, because the trick was to reward the quiet moments.

When Bear walked on stage, he didn't bark – until he noticed the audience, when he went off alarmingly. You can imagine. But after about a minute, he stopped barking for a couple of seconds, which was long enough for me to tell him what a good boy he was, in my most soothing voice. He soon started up again, but I did the same every time he took a break, and after about five minutes, he stopped barking altogether and plonked himself down, looking like he might doze off.

I must admit, I was quite surprised. Bear's owner thought I'd worked a miracle. Ten days later, she got in touch to tell me Bear hadn't barked on a walk since.

The classic situation, of course, is a dog barking at the post person. You know what the post person is up to, that they're just delivering letters, but your dog doesn't. He thinks they're a potential intruder, and that he makes the person go away by barking. That makes him feel good, because he thinks he's doing his job, which encourages him to keep doing it.

Even if you could talk to your dog and say, 'Mate, you've got it all wrong. She was gonna go away anyway without you barking, because she had more letters to deliver. Look! She's walking up to another house now. That's literally her job!' your dog would still reply, 'No, boss. What part of "I bark ... she runs away" don't you understand?'

The problem in that situation is that you can't take away the reward, because you still want to have letters delivered and we can hardly ask a busy postal worker to hang around five minutes until the dog stops barking. It's the same when dogs bark at things they see on the telly. Because while some dogs barely acknowledge the magic screen in the corner of the living room, others are transfixed by it. It's natural, when you think about it: why wouldn't they react to something small and furry running across a screen? And she probably started doing it when she was a puppy, when your reaction was, 'Oh look, she's barking at the telly! How cute!'

My old Rottie Axel never watched the telly, but Gordon did – he'd sit and watch it intently, his eyes darting left and right. The first time I was on the telly, Gordon heard my voice, looked at the telly, looked at me, looked back at the telly, looked back at me again, got up and walked right out of the room, probably thinking, 'How come there's two of him now? My brain can't cope with this ...'.

So, if you can't take away the reward, how do you fix it? Shouting doesn't work, and neither does shouting a bit louder, especially if you're doing it from the sofa. Your dog will just think you're joining in – backing him up – with trying to get rid of the intruders on the magic screen and start barking even more maniacally. Instead, get up and get between them and the screen. They might try to sidestep your legs, but swiftly re-block and say, 'No' (or whatever comes naturally, delivered in a calm and assertive – never aggressive – way). When they calm down for a couple of seconds, instead of muttering 'bloody dog' under your breath, tell him what a good boy he is. It might not be easy to switch from 'No' to 'Good boy, that's nice' in the blink of an eye, but that's the best way of getting your dog to understand.

If you're struggling, you might need to create a diluted version of the problem. Maybe record the TV advert that your dog keeps barking at and play it again and again. But – very important – start with the volume and brightness right down and turn them up, bit by bit. By starting with an easy version of the problem, you're giving both of you a chance. Eventually, the advert will be back at normal level and your dog will no longer be barking at it.

If your dog isn't barking in the house, maybe he keeps barking at something specific outside. I recently spoke to someone whose dog kept barking at trams. I understood the problem, because it happened to me once walking through Nottingham when I was working with a client and their dog. When you think about it, it's obvious why some dogs don't like trams: they make a loud rumbling noise and create vibrations through the ground. And in nature, when animals hear loud rumbling and feel the earth moving, they think, 'Best take cover. Something bad is happening.' But a dog can't take cover if she's on a lead.

Try to dilute the problem by taking her away from the trams. Maybe start on a side street adjacent to the main drag, along which the trams run, before switching to the training zone, where the dog is reacting a bit but not enough to send her over the edge. Then get nearer and nearer to the tram over time. It's OK to say 'No', as long as you're not shouty or nasty, and try to act as normal as possible, rather than thinking, 'Oh God, here we go, another tram . . .' (Because if you're acting stressed, we can hardly expect her to be calm, eh?) And, of course, when she doesn't react, give her plenty of soothing praise. We're aiming for her to see the tram and not react. We'll only achieve that by starting at a point where she's not in sensory overload.

It's probably a good time to mention a very different technique known as 'flooding', which involves immersing a dog (or a person) in a situation that scares them, 'dropping them in the deep end'. If it's a human who's afraid of spiders, for example, you might lock them in a room full of them. (I wouldn't personally, but then, I'm not an *I'm a Celebrity Get Me Out of Here* producer.) The problem with flooding is that while it may cure the patient (unlikely), it might make the issue even worse. Because there's a potential to do more harm than good, I consider it too risky.

Why do dogs bite?

The nipping that puppies do when they're teething and exploring the world through their mouths can be a bit annoying, but it's ultimately harmless. But when nipping turns into biting, it can potentially become very dangerous.

Only recently, I had my favourite tweed jacket almost ripped off my back by a Dobermann – he tore a whacking great hole in it and I was quite upset! You're probably thinking, 'Oh my God, that must have been a scary dog.' No, in fact, it was a dog who just wanted to play, and his idea of playing was using his chops.

If you've got a dog who is biting, whether it's playing or clearly being aggressive, and there's any chance that another dog or person can get hurt, seek professional advice. I can give you tips, but only by spending time with a dog can I understand what's making a dog bite and what, if anything, can be done about it. The last thing you want is for your dog to be upsetting and scaring people, or doing physical damage and landing themselves – and you – in trouble with the law.

Often dogs that bite are well trained and perfectly lovely with their own family, but suddenly turn into Mr Hyde with random strangers. Dogs bite out of fear; or because they're defending their territory or resource guarding (usually a bone or a toy); or if they're startled (which is why we're told to let sleeping dogs lie); or if they're in pain and lashing out (which is why a trip to the vet might be in order). Sometimes, they're trying to be bossy, and sometimes, like my Dobermann friend, they're just playing.

It might also depend on the breed: if you've got a collie that nips people's ankles, that's because they're mimicking the herding behaviour they were originally bred for.

People spend a lot of time trying to work out what triggers their dog's biting – was it a man or a woman? Were they wearing a hat? Were they carrying anything? – but my advice is to focus on the dog.

Any time somebody says to me, 'I've got this intermittent problem with my dog and it's driving me up the wall,' I turn that on its head and reply: 'Intermittent means that sometimes he's bad and you can't predict it, but it also means that sometimes he's good, which is when you need to praise him.' Because if you never praise the good thing, how does he know what you want from him? In cases of serious aggression that may not be enough. But at least it's a starting point.

In my first book, *All Dogs Great and Small*, I broke down how we communicate with dogs: through tone of voice, body language (including facial expressions) and touch. In other words, how we sound, how we look and how it feels.

If your dog is off her lead, facing away from you and nipping at people's ankles, you've only got your voice, which isn't terribly effective on its own from 50 yards away. You don't have body language, because the dog can't see you, and you certainly don't have touch. That's why I recommend using a long line while you're trying to fix the problem, because then you get touch back (via the harness or collar), as well as body language when she looks back at you.

Keep your dog at a safe distance from people you think are most likely to trigger his biting and if he looks like he's about to snap, tell him firmly, 'No', and if he manages to keep a lid on it, tell him, 'Good boy'. Over time, you can get closer and closer.

Some dogs have a habit of biting people and dogs in their own household, and it's often down to being backed into a corner (many humans will react in a similar manner). If you've got a nervous dog with a biting habit, make sure to give them an escape route. Don't walk towards them, so they think they can't get away, stand to one side and allow them to run past you.

People will often say to me, 'This bite came out of nowhere, it was completely out of character,' to which I'll usually reply,

'Are you absolutely sure there was nothing going on in the lead-up to the bite?' I ask that question because sometimes there is a build-up of tension that the owners don't notice.

I once met a couple whose German shepherd had bitten their daughter's friend. The dog had never done anything like that before, so they couldn't understand it. But it turned out that a couple of hours earlier, there had been a bit of a family emergency, which involved lots of phone calls, a lot of panic, and the dog being bundled into the car. When they all got back to the house, the daughter and her friend tried to squeeze through the narrow hallway at the same time as the dog, and the dog turned around and gave the daughter's friend a nip. It wasn't out of the blue at all; it had been building for a while.

Things that we think are cute, such as head strokes, hugs, putting your face in your dog's face and giving them a kiss, many dogs don't think are cute at all. And while some dogs will give warning signs – growling, whining, barking, lifting their top lip – others will just give a short look before biting (although if you know doggy body language, you'll probably have also seen them freeze).

I'm often asked how to protect you and your dog from an aggressive dog. The first thing to say is, if you come across a dog that gives you a bad feeling, you've got every right to give them a wide berth, so don't worry about coming across as anti-social. If a dog comes barrelling towards you and your dog, you have to make a judgement call. If it looks like it might escalate, calmly remove yourself, if possible, from the situation.

Try not to panic, which includes dragging your dog away by the collar, because that might heighten the tension. Instead, be decisive– 'No. That's enough now' – and friendly to the other dog's owner – 'Nice talking to you, see you soon.'

Dogs often bite simply because they're over-excited. One lady got in touch with me about her Staffie, whose excitement would lead to him biting visitors' wrists, which, in turn, unsurprisingly meant she no longer had visitors. She also had a two-year-old in the house, so she needed to resolve this issue sharpish.

This Staffie wasn't being vicious, he was just like a lot of Staffies, a ball of energy who liked exploring things with his mouth. Some dogs never grow out of that puppy habit and go through life thinking biting is just a great game.

Before I give anyone with a bitey dog training advice, I ask if the dog is getting enough physical and mental exercise. Do they let their dog stop and have a sniff on walks? Do you play mind-stimulating games with them? (Hiding treats around the living room is a really simple one.) Unless that stuff is already in place, any amount of training won't make much difference.

It's easier said than done, but try not to get excited when your dog is jumping up at people and biting, because if you do, things can quickly snowball. Try not to fling your arms around or say too much. By all means say no, but it's got to be authoritative, not shouty (because good bosses don't have to shout). You can try putting the dog in 'time out', maybe in the kitchen behind a gate, but you can't let them back into the living room until they've cooled down. The reward for being calm is rejoining the family, and if he goes back to being a silly-billy, put him straight back into the kitchen. And repeat. Everything has to be done with calm, not angry energy, whether it's a feeling of 'Good boy, back in,' or 'You blew it. Out you go again.'

Some owners will throw their dog a bone to calm them down, but that's not dealing with the root cause, and bones keep some dogs excited. Manhandling can also be a problem, because dogs have a level of excitement past which they can't think straight. If you grab him by the collar and try to drag him away, he'll likely bite you because he literally can't think straight at that moment.

I once worked with a Jack Russell called Titch. Before I turned up, he kept biting his mum and dad, and it was getting worse and worse.

Titch was ninja quick and didn't just nip, he properly bit – and he was doing it multiple times a day. It was really getting his mum and dad down. The only way they could move him outside was to usher him into a crate and move him that way. But that was making the problem even worse, because as soon as he saw them coming with it, he knew that he was about to be captured.

Very quickly I spotted that while the couple were scared of Titch, he was also scared of *them*, which made them feel quite sad. So instead of them going towards him, I suggested they encourage him to come to them. I got them to use pieces of chicken and drop them closer and closer to them, and by the end of the session, Titch was happy to jump on the sofa between his mum and dad. Touchingly, it was the closest they'd been able to sit with their dog in a couple of years.

It doesn't matter how big your dog is, because even if he's a Jack Russell, Chihuahua or a dachshund, you're going to know about it if he gives you a nip. Thankfully, there are things you can do to prevent it from happening.

It's never about forcing your dog to do things he doesn't want to – that's not leadership. It's about creating conditions in which your dog wants to follow you and leaving him wanting more.

Why do dogs eat poo?

This is not a subject that often comes up at dinner parties, but it is a surprisingly common habit among dogs. According to the Kennel Club, about 25 per cent of dogs eat poo – known as coprophagia – and they do so for a variety of reasons.

In the wild, canine mums eat their puppies' poo to keep their dens clean and stop predators being drawn to the smell, and the puppies will copy their mum's behaviour. Others eat poo because they're bored and have nothing else to do, for example if they're stuck at home on their own all day. And others do it because they have a medical condition, such as worms or diabetes.

But here's the kicker: some dogs eat poo simply because they're hungry and they like it. Gross, I know. Their powerful noses are able to decipher all sorts of undigested matter that tastes yummy to them – fats, proteins and other material – which is a hunting skill. On top of that, commercial dog food has a strong smell when it goes in and it's still there when it comes out the other end! So when he sniffs his number twos, he doesn't think, 'Ugh, dog poo!' he thinks, 'Lovely jubbly, there's more of that beef and liver in there somewhere . . .'

Not so long ago, I heard from the owner of a cockapoo who was at her wits' end because he kept eating his poos during the night and she didn't want it to become a habit.

I was pretty sure it was going to fix itself anyway, because that's what normally happens when puppies become adults.

But I understood his owner's concern and embarrassment, not least because everybody else you know carries on as if their puppy is perfect!

My solution was to feed the little lad less for his evening meal and give it to him earlier, so that he had plenty of opportunities to evacuate before bedtime. That way, his owner could be there when he went to the toilet in the garden and get rid of it before he had a chance to gobble it up. And if you get distracted and your dog does try to eat it, it's OK to tell them off, but – as ever – not in a nasty way. A calm 'no', said once to mark the unwanted behaviour, and while they are doing it, is enough.

As I say, most puppies grow out of it, just as human teenagers grow out of all sorts of filthy habits, but some don't. I once met a chocolate Labrador who'd wake up in the middle of the night, do a number two on the rug, pick it up and take it to her bed. She'd have a quick nibble and save a bit for later, as if she was rationing a chocolate bar, so when her owners came downstairs in the morning, the poo would be all over the Labrador and all over her bed. It didn't help that the poo was brown, the dog was brown and the bed ... well ... you get the picture. (I do hope you're not reading this while you're eating ...)

Why do dogs lick?

Most dogs lick, but some dogs lick more than others. Take my two Rottweilers, Axel and Gordon. Axel was one of those dogs who didn't really care if you loved him or not. He quite liked being stroked and the rest of it, but if I didn't pay him attention, it wouldn't bother him. But Gordon, who was Axel's nephew, and only a year younger, was a completely different character.

Gordon would lick people left, right and centre. When he met someone, he'd bound towards them and stick his face in their face, which frightened the life out of some people. I wasn't known as a dog expert back then, so when I came out with the classic, 'Don't worry, he likes you!' they were inclined not to believe me. Only when Gordon started licking them all over did they realise it was his way of saying, 'Please love me! Please tell me you love me!' He looked scary to some people, understandably, but in truth he was as soft as mushy peas.

Dogs, like a lot of mammals, lick instinctively. They lick to groom. Mothers lick their puppies to clean and comfort them, as well as prompt them to go to the toilet. Wild dog puppies lick their mother's lips to indicate they're hungry. But mostly mothers and puppies – and littermates – lick each other simply as a sign of affection.

Some say a dog licks his owner as a sign of submission, but I'm more inclined to say that a dog who licks a lot is just a bit needy. It's all part of the glorious bond between dog and owner, which is why when people say, 'Can you please get my dog to lick less?' I'm sometimes a bit reluctant, because you don't really want to suppress a dog's natural need to demonstrate affection. Multiple studies have shown that licking releases endorphins and dopamine in a dog's brain, which makes them feel calmer and more relaxed. There are limits though, of course.

When you stroke a strange dog, he might lick your hand, which is his way of saying hello back. When your dog licks under your chin, or around your mouth, that might be him telling you he fancies something to eat. Alternatively a dog might lick you if it thinks you're not well, emotionally or physically: a 2012 study by researchers at Goldsmiths, University of London, asked owners to pretend to cry, and found that dogs were more likely to lick and nuzzle them than when they were humming or talking, which might suggest they were showing empathy.

We also just taste good to dogs, because of certain glands located in different parts of our body – soles of the feet, palms, forehead, cheeks and armpits and ear canals (apparently the smell of our earwax triggers a dog's sense of taste). But all those adverts you see on the telly that make out your dog's taste is as refined as a Michelin-starred chef are very misleading.

While humans have about 9,000 taste buds on their tongues, dogs only have about 1,700, which means our taste is about six times more powerful than theirs. Cats, by the way, only have about 470, which makes their food ads even more silly!

Dogs have the same four main taste classifications as us – sweet, sour, salty and bitter – but in common with lots of other carnivores, they also have bonus taste buds evolved specifically for water. They're in the tip of the tongue and are more sensitive after eating sweet and salty foods. If only we humans could taste water, then perhaps we wouldn't be tempted to drink fattening fizzy pop!

The $64,000 question is why do dogs eat anything from steak to their own poo if their sense of taste isn't actually that bad? Well, that's because a dog's smell is far more powerful, and they actually have a special bit of kit called the vomeronasal organ that enables them to smell and taste simultaneously.

Primarily, dogs use the vomeronasal organ to smell pheromones, or chemical signals, given off by other dogs, which helps them work out whether they're happy, scared or in the mood for mating. But it's also what enables them to differentiate between meat-based and non-meat-based foods, and why the more pungent something smells to a dog, the more enticing it is. As such, if your dog keeps turning his nose up at kibble, maybe try wet food instead, because some of that stuff really pongs. Tripe, monsieur . . . ? Delicious!

Some people are of the opinion that letting a dog lick you anywhere is a bit icky. I do have a degree of sympathy when it comes to a dog licking you on the face, especially the mouth, because you're never quite sure where that tongue has been! If you are a bit squeamish, you can dissuade them; the easiest way to do so is to turn your face, stand up and walk away, in the manner of somebody saying, 'Sorry, mate, you wanted affection, but now you've blown it.'

What you're trying to communicate is that while a cuddle and a bit of nuzzling is OK, as soon as they go in for a lick, you're not going to stand for it. Sooner or later they'll make the connection: 'Oh, right. He's nice when I nuzzle, so that must be OK. But if I get the old tongue out, I lose out. I'll be doing that a lot less now . . .' Consistency, as with most things dog-training related, is key.

Why do dogs hump?

If you've got a dog who keeps humping other dogs, people's legs and even inanimate objects, never fear, he's probably not a sex maniac. Such friskiness is perfectly normal in dogs and, as with humans, kicks in when they're young, when testosterone starts surging through their bodies. (Although some females do it too, see below.)

Humping isn't necessarily a sexual thing; it might just be that the dog is over-excited or is trying to exert themselves over another dog or human. But there is plenty of evidence that suggests lots of mammals get pleasure from sex.

While humping is completely natural, it can be embarrassing for owners. And if it's a mastiff who likes humping people's legs, it can be borderline dangerous.

Most visitors having their leg humped will be very polite, and some will even laugh. When I ask people what their reaction was when their dog first started humping legs, they almost all reply, 'We thought it was funny to start with.' Some of them even got their phones out and started filming. But essentially humping is super-charged attention seeking, and laughing and filming will only encourage it. The very worst thing the humpee can do is jiggle their leg about, because the dog will interpret that as enjoyment and/or praise. They'll be looking around as if to say, 'They love it! They absolutely love it!'

Most dogs, like teenage boys, become less hot to trot and less likely to hump with time. But getting an amorous dog neutered won't necessarily stop this behaviour, because while that does reduce testosterone levels, the habit might remain in a dog that's been happily humping for years.

I've met many dogs of many breeds (including a few female ones) who would hump anything in sight – vacuum cleaners, toys, mops, the neighbours' legs, the list is endless. You name something, I've probably seen a dog hump it.

When it happens, the dog is usually very young, and it can be quite funny. Everyone points at the dog and has a giggle, and any self-respecting dog will probably realise that they're the centre of attention and that the secret to becoming the star of the show is to do the humpy thing. So if you've got a dog who's humping something, however bizarre the item might be, the principle is always the same: you need to nip it in the bud as quickly as possible – especially if you have a big dog – and telling him off is fine, as long as your tone is stern but calm. Better still if you reward the moment when he decides to back away.

Let's take the example of a dog who's humping a broom. I'd put myself between him and the broom, calmly telling him 'off' before he gets into full swing. When he backs off, gently tell him what a good boy he is. After just a few minutes, he should soon realise two things: he's getting more attention and affection for backing off and a broom isn't a potential future partner.

Surprisingly, female dogs hump as well, although in their case it's about showing who's boss. So you might see a male and female dog playing rowdily and the female dog will grab and hump the male dog, almost like a wrestling move. That's the female dog saying, 'Don't get above your station, I think you'll find that I'm above you in the pecking order around these parts.'

Why do dogs shake and shiver?

If your dog is shivering or trembling, it doesn't necessarily mean they're cold. It could mean lots of things, including excitement, pain, nausea and old age. But the most likely reason is plain old nervousness. I'm inclined to believe it's the dog's brain trying to work out a situation when they can't decide what to do – 'Run away . . . go forward . . . run away . . . go forward . . . ?' – although there's no science to prove that. Yet.

Then there's the shake-off, which is when your dog looks like he's trying to fling water off his fur when he's not wet. You'll have seen your dog shake off immediately after waking up, often combined with a full-body stretch. That's probably just him shaking off the grogginess and reinvigorating the body, just as a human would do after a good sleep.

Your dog may also shake off after meeting another dog in the park, or after getting a whiff of something unusual, which is probably him trying to let go of anxiety – 'Phew, that wasn't as bad as I thought it might be.' It's the canine equivalent of a human dropping their shoulders in relief. Dogs also shake off after running around like lunatics or when they're coming down from an excited state – your dog might do it just before leaving the house for a walk, and he might also do it after getting home, which is him literally shaking off energy and becoming calm again.

So don't worry if your dog shakes off a lot – which most dogs do – it's actually a good chance to tell him what a good boy he is for calming down.

Why do dogs lunge?

When it comes to dogs, reactivity refers to any sight, sound or smell that triggers an unwanted behaviour, whether it's barking, growling, pulling on the lead or lunging.

Some dogs will have been fine until something happened in their life, whether it was being attacked by another dog who scared the bejesus out of him or spooked by a police siren. But the good thing is, if a behaviour has been learnt, it can potentially be unlearnt.

Dogs lunging at traffic is a very common issue, whether it's a pushbike, motorbike, a backfiring car, or a roaring lorry that triggers it. Usually what's happening is the dog is lunging at traffic to get rid of it. And because whatever it is usually drives away, they think they've done their job. It can cause owners a lot of anxiety, because some dogs will run straight at anything, even an articulated lorry. And once they start to lose the plot, they can start reacting to and lunging at everything, whether it's a crisp packet on the wind or a pigeon taking flight (spaniels, I'm looking at YOU).

Sometimes, it gets so bad that owners are afraid to walk their dog next to roads, which can be quite difficult if you live in a town or city, like most people. In extreme cases, an owner might stop taking their dog out altogether.

First things first: make sure you've got a collar or harness that you can trust completely, so that you can at least feel more confident in being able to safely restrain your dog. Behind the ears is the most effective place for a collar, and if you've opted for a harness, make sure it fits snugly, for two reasons: first, your dog won't be able to slip out of it; second, it can have a swaddling effect, in that it feels like a light cuddle (you can also buy special T-shirts for that purpose,).

The trick with a dog who lunges at traffic is to start the training somewhere a bit further away from the main road and gradually take her closer over time. You can also introduce a nudge down the lead, which will act like a tap on the shoulder and a quiet word in her ear: 'Mate, I'm talking to you.' If that's not enough for her to back down, step in front of her, the message being, 'You're going to have to get through me to get to that lorry. Back off.' She'll probably sidestep you the first couple of times – 'Out of the way, I'm trying to make that lorry go away!' – but when she does back down, make sure to praise her with your voice and hands. Dogs won't usually take treats in that situation, because they're so nervous, in much the same way a person won't eat when they're really nervous.

YOu'll often get dogs who are fine off the lead but always lunging and barking on it, and that's probably because they feel restricted. If a dog is off the lead, she can give herself room and take her time. If she wants to go and say hello to another dog, she can. If she doesn't, no problem. But if she's attached to this great big human, she'll feel less free and lacking in options.

That said, you do need to be able to keep your dog under control on a lead. This can cause problems for reactive dogs, especially if they encounter a potentially hostile dog while they are out and about. We've all seen how this plays out. If another dog comes towards her, she'll slip straight into fight mode, because the flight option isn't open to her. She'll lunge and bark to get the other dog to back off and give her a bit of space. Meanwhile, the owner will usually be pulling their dog back, which exaggerates the body language, meaning the other dog will be thinking, 'Blimey, that dog is really straining for a fight. Come on then!' That's when things can get a bit ugly.

The best thing to do if your dog lunges at another dog/ person/cyclist etc. is not to go in the direction of the lunge, which often happens, but carry on walking in a straight line (although that doesn't mean kneeing your dog in the head if they lunged across in front of you!). Also, keep the lead slack, with a J shape at the bottom, and not too long. Dogs are like most animals, in that as soon as they feel tension, they will pull in the other direction.

Why do dogs jump up?

Let's face it, dogs jumping up at people can be quite cute. It usually starts in puppyhood, and it looks lovely, because it's basically a dog who's really excited and wants you to give them attention. But, at the risk of sounding like a killjoy, it should probably be discouraged, for various reasons.

My general rule is, four paws on the floor makes them a good boy or girl, unless you're training them to jump through hoops of fire or some such.

For starters, nobody wants laddered tights or muddy paws all over their pristine white trousers, especially not some poor person minding their own business in the high street. But more than that, dogs jumping up can be terrifying for people, even those who like dogs, especially small children.

Puppies start jumping up because it's a good way of getting attention from their owners. And because it looks cute, their owners encourage it by grabbing the dog's paws, stroking him on the head, smiling and telling him what a good boy he is. Consequently, the puppy does it even more. Then, a few months down the line, all that jumping up has become a bit annoying, embarrassing even. And if your dog is a big 'un, it could get you into trouble – even if you're shouting, 'Don't worry, he's friendly!' while he's doing it. (Been there, done that, seen the error of my ways!)

If you've got a dog who keeps jumping up at people, you can try to ignore the behaviour, which we spoke about earlier in relation to attention seeking. The problem with ignoring is that it has to be absolute, meaning that everybody your dog jumps up at will need to ignore it too, otherwise it won't do the trick. And that's very unlikely to happen when strangers and children are involved.

The other option is to try to make your dog feel uncomfortable by saying no. But remember, the tone of voice has to be right. If you sound too excited – 'God! No! Stop it! No!' – you might as well be saying, 'Jump! Jump! Jump!' Whereas if the look on your face when you say no signals the message 'I don't think so, young man,' your body language will follow.

You can also use touch, but I don't mean pushing him back down, because his backside will just pre-load with muscular tension and he'll spring straight back up again, which is the greatest game known to dog. Instead, just nudge them off to the side, although not with the aim of knocking him over. Four-legged animals are designed to jump and land with both paws hitting the ground at the same time, so landing on one paw will make him feel a little bit off-balance.

If you get the sound, look and touch right, your dog will hopefully be thinking, 'Whoa, that didn't feel right.' And when he's sitting there weighing things up, that's when you need to give him plenty of gentle praise – 'Oh, good boy, that's nice' – and if you do touch him, it should be long, slow strokes, otherwise you risk revving him up again.

If you've got a dog who keeps jumping up at kitchen work surfaces while food is being prepared, brush him off-balance (brush, not shove!), tell him 'Off', but only reward him with a treat in his bowl if he stays down for a reasonable amount of time, otherwise he'll just keep popping back up. Bit by bit, extend the amount of time before you chuck him a treat, and eventually you can make it random – what we call a variable reward schedule. That way, he won't know when you're going to chuck him a treat, so will think, 'OK, if I stay down here, there'll probably be something in it for me at some stage ...'

Another training technique for dogs who jump up at kitchen work surfaces is to set a trap for him, by which I mean leave some food up there on purpose and watch him through a crack in the door. Just when your dog looks like he's thinking, 'I'm going to jump up there and steal that sausage. I ... just ... can't ... resist,' walk around the corner and say 'No'. The dog will probably look around all confused, which can be quite funny – but try not to giggle, because your face needs to be like thunder. Don't worry, you can switch to Mr Nice Guy/Girl when he behaves himself. The important thing here is that you're not being nasty in your demeanour, more 'I am SO disappointed in you!' You know that feeling when, as a kid, you thought your mum had eyes in the back of her head – how did she know you'd just been naughty ...? That's what we're after.

Why do dogs wag their tails?

Ask almost anybody why dogs wag their tails, including dog owners, and they'll say, 'Because they're happy.' Or if you do it the other way round and say, 'Describe a happy dog,' the first thing they'll say is, waggy tail! However, tail wagging is a bit more complicated than that ...

A dog wagging her tail could well be happy, but she could be wagging her tail for another reason. You've got to look at the whole picture. If she's doing what I would describe as a full-body wag, hips and all, and you've just walked through the door after work, chances are she is just happy as Larry. But a waggy tail is just a sign of excitement – and excitement comes in lots of different flavours.

A dog might be wagging her tail because she's thinking, 'I'm getting a bit excited and it's going to tip over in a minute' (remember when you were a kid and your mum would say to you, 'Oi! Pack it in or it'll turn to crying'?). And I've also seen dogs wagging their tails just before attacking. German shepherds who work as police dogs sometimes do a slower tail wag – big, long swishes – when they're weighing up the perfect time to lunge at someone or something. The rest of the dog's body will be very stiff, ready to pounce, unlike the full-body wag I described above.

Different breeds have tails of all different shapes and sizes, while some dogs might not have a tail at all. There are 34 bobtail breeds, as they're properly called, including the English and French bulldog and the Boston terrier – and obviously some unfortunate dogs lose their tails due to injury. But don't worry if someone has told you a dog with no tail can't communicate properly; as long as they're well socialised, they'll be fine, because dogs look at the whole picture.

My two Rotties didn't have tails, because they were born before the docking ban came in and it was nigh on impossible to find one with a tail. But I could still spot when their tail was wagging, because the stump still moved. In fact, I once entered Gordon into a waggiest tail competition and he won! (Kids would ask what happened to his tail and I'd tell them he wagged it so much it fell off. I thought that was quite funny, until one day I said it to a little boy and he started crying. Oops. I stopped using that line after that.)

Why do dogs dig?

Some dogs are optimists; they'll get a whiff of something and just dig, dig, dig, on the off-chance that something interesting is under there.

If you've got a terrier or a small hound, they're just doing what they were bred to do, which was dig quarry from their dens. Digging might also relieve stress and boredom, while some dogs might be dredging up cold earth to cool off with if it's hot.

Another reason dogs dig is to retrieve something they've hidden, usually a bone. You'll sometimes see them digging at a cushion on the sofa or at the carpet in the corner of the living room, because, unbeknown to you, that's where they've hidden a chew. Dogs hide things for the same reason their ancestors hid things in the wild: they've eaten as much as they can right now but still have some left and don't want another dog to find it. Unfortunately, when modern dogs dig up old bones, they sometimes end up on the kitchen floor, much to the disapproval of a houseproud owner.

But mostly, dogs dig because it makes them feel good, which is why we shouldn't worry about it unless they're turning your garden into a bombsite.

A lot of dogs grow out of digging, but if yours hasn't and you want to stop him putting great big holes in your lawn, make a sand or gravel pit, because it seems cruel to stop a dog with a strong instinct from digging altogether. To make it more fun and rewarding, you can hide a toy in the pit, which you'll probably be less annoyed to find in the kitchen.

However, a pit won't solve the problem on its own. You'll also need to supervise, because she will get bored of digging in the pit eventually and head back to the lawn, thinking she'll find a toy there as well. Whenever she does that, tell her no, while maybe blocking the potential dig site with your foot, before leading her back to the sandpit and rewarding her. Keep doing that until the message sinks in.

Why do dogs stare?

In one of my previous books, I wrote about my encounter with dingoes on K'gari (formerly Fraser Island), which is off the coast of Queensland.

Dingoes aren't wolves, but they're not domestic dogs either. In fact, scientists are still arguing about what exactly dingoes are, but it's widely accepted that they're an ancient lineage of dog. For that reason, I thought they might be able to give me some insight into why our pet dogs behave the way they do.

Like many wild animals, dingoes can be dangerous; they can take down cattle and kangaroos and do a lot of damage to humans. So when my Indigenous friend advised me not to take my eyes off a dingo should one wander into our path, I was taken aback, because I'd been taught never to stare out an aggressive dog. Then he told me not to look away, either, because they'd think I was weak and attack.

I was somewhat baffled, until my friend made clear that by not taking my eyes off the dingo, he actually meant looking in its general direction rather than staring straight into its eyes. His other advice was to stand my ground and take my time, the point being that either extreme – staring the dingo out or nervously looking away – would likely provoke an attack. As with many things in life, the middle ground was the way. Although my friend was speaking from personal experience (and thousands of years' worth of collective wisdom of the Butchulla people, the traditional owners of K'gari), I'm thankful I never had to put it into practice myself.

Not long after I'd returned to England, a family from London got in touch to tell me they had a Rottweiler who wouldn't let any visitors into the house. He wasn't great outside, either.

While my own two Rotties were both lovely dogs, I knew they could be pretty scary. Sure enough, when I turned up at this house, it sounded like a rabid animal from hell was behind the door.

We'd arranged for the dog to be on a muzzle, but I was still a bit edgy. And when his owners let him out of a side room, he ran up to me, barking like crazy, and started bouncing off my hip. Good job he had that muzzle on, because otherwise he would have taken a chunk out of me. The good thing was, I could finally put my dingo technique into practice. And hope it worked.

I stood my ground, looked in his general direction and did my best not to look terrified, which was easier said than done. And after two or three minutes (which seemed like an eternity!), his barking and rabid snarling gave way to less urgent ruffs, which was his way of saying, 'All this aggro doesn't seem to be working with this guy.'

The dog was no longer 100 per cent focused on me; in fact he kept looking at his bed. And eventually, he fell completely silent and took himself off there, with a big, comical harrumph. After about an hour, he approached me and I was able to stroke him (without staring at him, I should add). He'd accepted that I wasn't a threat, but I wasn't a pushover either. After that, we went for a walk around the park, without any issues. It was one of those turnarounds that I couldn't entirely have predicted, but was very grateful for. At the end of the consultation, his owners said, 'He's like a different dog.' I love hearing that! And all due to a chance conversation at the other end of the world about wild dogs . . .

So that's what I call the dingo technique, and it works with lots of animals. Push too far and the animal will feel threatened and is likely to come out fighting. Back off, and he will think you're a soft touch and go for you. Somewhere in between is the sweet spot. The dingo technique comes with a caveat: don't try this at home, kids, unless you're in trouble and it's a last resort. It's the best way I know of defusing an aggressive dog, but it doesn't come with a guarantee. You may still be bitten. I can't stress enough that if you're worried about aggression from your dog, you should seek professional help.

But most dogs aren't much different to humans when it comes to staring. We're all told it's rude to stare when we're kids, and if someone keeps staring at you in everyday life – maybe down the pub or on the Tube – you're eventually going to feel quite uncomfortable. You're probably more likely to avert your gaze than confront the starer, to avoid any potential conflict (because you're a nice person, right?), and dogs usually do the same, especially if you stare at them from close range. That's your dog saying, 'Sorry, sorry, I don't want to start anything …'. It follows then that you shouldn't force the issue. You'll also notice that when two dogs meet, they'll often turn their heads away from each other.

But staring isn't always a negative thing with dogs. In fact, dogs stare at humans for all sorts of reasons, but usually because they want to know or communicate something. They might simply want to know what you're up to and what you're going to do next. Your behaviour might be confusing them ('I don't know what you want me to do! Give me another hint!') or they might think you want something from them when you don't. They might want food, a walk or to go to the toilet. Or they might just want to play and/or a cuddle!

If your dog is staring at you, they're essentially reading you. They're trying to decode your body language and facial expressions, to understand what you're thinking or feeling. Remember, your dog relies on you for almost everything, so they're constantly trying to decipher your actions, whether it's putting on your shoes ('Is she taking me out for a walk?') or opening the fridge ('Oh aye? Is she going to give me a piece of sausage?').

The opposite to staring is blinking. When a dog's nervous or unsure, they often stop blinking (that is, they start staring), because their brain is busy thinking about running away or fighting. Humans do the same, as we know from the phrase 'He was so scared, his eyes were like dinner plates.' If a strange dog keeps staring at you, try blinking back at it, because that's you saying, 'Hey, I'm not staring, I come in peace.' What usually happens, although maybe not immediately, is that the dog will blink back. That's a great bit of human–dog communication and it's lovely when it happens. The power of blinking . . . who knew, eh?

Why do dogs walk in circles?

We don't really know why dogs circle before hitting the hay or going to the toilet – and not all dogs do – but some clever people have come up with plenty of suggestions.

One theory is that circling goes back to dogs' early ancestors, who would have flattened rough ground into a more comfortable sleeping area before retiring for the night. You might have seen your dog do something similar in his bed while digging at his blankets, which the experts think harks back to when wild dogs checked for small, potentially dangerous, creatures, such as snakes and spiders.

Circling before going to the toilet would have allowed wild dogs to pick up the scent of potential predators – squatting animals are quite vulnerable – which might explain why some modern dogs circle several times before deciding to do their business, or choosing to do it only somewhere where they feel more secure. Flattening the grass also makes the area 'cleaner', in that there's less chance of their poo getting smeared on long grass and getting stuck to their backsides.

Another theory is that dogs circle before doing their business, and sometimes kick the ground with their hind legs afterwards, to mark their territory (dogs have scent glands on their paw pads). Then there's the theory that a dog circles simply to get his bowels moving.

I've even heard it said that dogs circle to align themselves with a certain compass point every time. I'm not sure about that one, but I'm not about to launch a study – life's too short to be getting a compass, pen and notepad out every time my dogs go for a poo. Don't let me stop you though, and do let me know your findings!

Some smaller female dogs do handstands while urinating. Very impressive! One such dog was a Boston terrier I knew called Doris, who was probably trying to cover urine left by bigger dogs. Or maybe she saw the look on her owner's face the first time she did it, which was probably one of amusement, and thought, 'Ah, they like that, I'll do it for them again . . .'

It sounds far-fetched, but I'm convinced dogs do stuff just to entertain us. Someone once told me their dog does a moonwalk before he drinks water from his bowl. This dog would jump off the sofa, walk three or four feet, stop, look at Mum and Dad, then break into his Michael Jackson impersonation. When I asked how she and her partner reacted, she said they laughed every time. There's no doubt in my mind that if you could ask that dog why he did it, he'd say, 'I don't know. But everybody loves it. Here, watch me do it again . . .'

Some male dogs never cock their legs to wee (which it's said is normally done to get the spray as high as possible and cover the scent of other dogs: 'Bonzo woz 'ere!'), and that's perhaps because they were neutered quite young and never developed the hormones that told them to do it. Male dogs who squat to wee tend to be more submissive characters – they don't feel moved to rewrite history with urine! And you can get female dogs who cock their legs, although that's quite rare. But whatever their technique, it's probably nothing to worry about. Like humans, dogs have their little quirks. (And isn't the world a better place for it?)

Chapter 6

Different Dogs

We can tinker all we like with dogs; coax them into brain scanners to understand more; persuade them as best we can to behave themselves, armed with all the latest findings and methods; dress them up in jumpers and bow ties. But dogs are, and always will be, more wolf than human.

Domesticated animals are still animals, so they'll never lose all their natural instincts. And, as we have seen, dogs are all individuals, so not all of them will fit snugly into a world shaped by humans. There will be the non-conformists, the malcontents and the simply not as smart as we'd desperately like them to be.

In a way, that's great, because the world would be a far less colourful place if all dogs behaved themselves (and I'd be out of a job). But there is such a thing as too much misbehaving, and there are dogs who don't even like to do what dogs are 'meant' to do, like fetch balls and hang around with humans.

Sometimes that's a problem, sometimes it's not. But things can usually be fixed, or made smooth. And, I should stress, there's nothing really 'wrong' with a dog who isn't big on fetching balls or hanging around with humans, they're just a bit different.

Then there are the dogs with disabilities, which might only be disabilities to us. I've met plenty of dogs who were missing an eye, a limb or something else – I've got one who's blind and one who's deaf! – and they don't want a human's sympathy, they just want to crack on with life as normal. Normal for them.

Why doesn't my dog like toys?

People often think their dog might be misbehaving in the house because they're not getting enough physical exercise, but mental exercise is just as important, especially if you've got a working breed, such as a collie or poodle.

Toys and games are fun for dogs, in the same way as they're fun for children. Puppies just love running around with something in their mouths, or fighting over a favourite toy (aka your slipper) with another puppy, and they learn very early on that if they bring their owner a toy, or a ball, they'll make it come alive, by wiggling it around or throwing it. And most puppies will love that so much that they'll want you to wiggle it around and throw it over and over again.

Toys are also brilliant training rewards and a great way of keeping your dog mentally stimulated. However, I've come across plenty of dogs who don't seem to be interested in toys at all, which some owners find difficult.

You might have imagined spending hours over the park playing fetch, but your dog just looks at the ball and wanders off in the opposite direction. 'Well, you threw it. Go fetch it yourself, fool!' Perhaps you had dreams of training your dog to do all sorts of amazing toy-related tricks. And maybe you're thinking, 'If he doesn't want to play with toys, does that mean he's unhappy?' But it doesn't really work like that.

Some dogs never stop playing with toys, from the time they're born to the time they shuffle off to the great kennel in the sky. Our boxer is 13, which is old for the breed, and still brings toys over. He doesn't really want us to play, he just wants to prove that he can still snatch it quicker than us. And some dogs become obsessed with toys, Border collies and spaniels spring to mind (excuse the pun). In fact, you might want to limit the number of times you accede to some dogs' demand to throw the ball, because they might never want to stop.

Other dogs are more motivated by food than toys. You'll show them a toy and they'll give you a look that says, 'Nah. I can't be bovvered with that.' I'd probably look at you the same if you offered me some spinach as a reward (though offer me a £10 note or a custard cream and I'm all yours).

If your dog is a rescue, it might be the case that he never learnt to play with toys as a puppy, or maybe he accidentally bit his owner while playing with a toy and was harshly punished for it. Saying that, rescue dogs often take a bit of time to come out of their shell, and they might start playing with toys after a few months.

So don't beat yourself up if your dog doesn't want to play ball, there are other ways of training him and keeping his big brain ticking over. And a dog who really isn't into toys won't thank you for forcing him to play with them.

However, some reluctant dogs can be taught – even Rottweilers, who are famously stubborn. Which reminds me of a joke:

What would different dogs say if you asked them to change a lightbulb?

Border collie: 'Right, I've changed the lightbulb. Do you want me to check the wiring as well?'

Boxer: 'We don't need to change the lightbulb, I can play with my toys in the dark.'

Rottweiler: 'Make me.'

Back to teaching dogs to play. Maybe get one of those balls on a rope (a sturdy one if you have a large dog such as a Rottweiler, because Rotties can kill a tennis ball in seconds) and leave it lying around. Sooner or later, she'll pick it up, and when she does, try to take it away from her with the rope part. Then it could be game on.

Don't overdo things, otherwise you'll rev her up and teach her to be possessive. Having played for a few seconds, go still – be a post – and as soon as she opens her mouth to drop it, say 'out' (you could say 'drop' or 'leave', but I think 'out' sounds authoritative and a bit like a bark), before telling her what a good girl she is and – importantly – giving it straight back to her. Her reward for letting go is to get it straight back. Instead of thinking, 'If I let go, they'll take it away,' we're training her to believe the opposite: 'If I let go, they give it straight back and we play again. There's literally no downside to letting go of things.' Add to that your new prompt ('Out/drop/leave') and you have a system for life. The first attempt might take a while, incidentally – I once did a consultation with a Rottie and had to hold on for 20 minutes!

By giving the ball back to them you're rewarding them with the thing they want most, on condition they willingly drop it. Don't keep letting them win (especially if it's a powerful dog), because that will just teach them to hang on for dear life to anything they get their teeth into. You also need to make sure you time your 'out' command with when she opens her mouth to drop it, because if you do it before, she'll think it means carry on clamping, because dogs associate human word prompts with whatever they are doing at that precise moment.

Eventually, she'll connect your praise and reward with the fact she's dropped the ball, and further down the line, when she picks up something you really don't want her to pick up, like one of your children's toys or a slipper, you can tell her 'out' and she'll drop it, knowing there's something in it for her.

As mentioned earlier, a quick google for 'canine enrichment' will throw up all sorts of things, and there are lots of simple games you can play with your dog to keep her brain ticking over. And if your dog is more motivated by food than toys, there are crafty ways of combining the two.

A good way of engaging your dog's brain is to play hide and seek with treats, because the proportion of a dog's brain given over to smell is massive compared to ours.

Tracking is another good one. Make a set of footprints in the ground and place a treat at the toe end of each one as you go. Then, at the end of each trail, set down a little bit of food in a container that he needs you to open – the pot of gold, if you will. Once you've laid your track, walk away from the end at a right angle and loop back to the beginning to avoid laying confusing extra tracks on the ground. Now walk the trail with your dog. He'll sniff the footprints, smell you and your foot, as well as the stamped blades of grass, and you'll see his head going left, right, left, right. And at the end – jackpot! This activity is great because you're working as a team, which is good for bonding, and as time goes on you can make the trail longer, and maybe add in a few bends, so that maybe he loses the scent and locks back on to it. All dogs can do it, and most dogs love it.

For more bonding, brain training and general happiness, try putting the treat inside a small container (I used to use those little canisters that camera film came in, before everything went digital, but anything similar will do) and punch a few small holes in it, so that the smell comes out. I recommend something pungent like a bit of cream cheese or some pâté. The container should be one that your dog can't open for themself. They will desperately want to get to that treat, and eventually think, 'I know what, I'll get a handy human to do it for me . . .' When she brings it to you, you can tell her what a good girl she is, stick your finger in and feed her the treat. It's a team game!

There are lots of brain-training ideas out there that don't require more traditional toys, like a ball, frisbee or rubber bone, including dog puzzles that you can load with treats. But in most cases, you needn't be obsessed with keeping your dog entertained at all hours of the day. As long as most dogs are well fed, well walked and have a cosy place to sleep, they'll be happy.

Why is my dog so greedy?

I'm not really one to talk about weight, because I'm perhaps a tad heftier than I ought to be. (It's those pesky custard creams.)

Having said that, there's almost never a good excuse for your dog to be overweight.

You might assume that overweight people are more likely to have overweight dogs, but quite often I see a chubby dog with a slim owner. That's presumably because, while they're disciplined with their own diet, they're a sucker for puppy-dog eyes: 'Oh, go on then, have half my dinner . . .'

We've got to remember that we're in control of what our dogs eat, just as we're in control of what our children eat. You might think that having a Labrador is a get-out-of-jail-free card, because we know their tendency to be overweight is, to some extent, genetic. Back in 2016, scientists from Cambridge University reported that 23 per cent of Labradors carry a mutant form of a gene called POMC, which means they never feel full (amazingly, this mutation affects humans in the same way). I'm not going to argue with the science, but what I will say is, to turn the logic on its head, three-quarters of Labradors AREN'T affected by that mutation – and the vast majority of Labradors can't open fridge doors. I'm afraid if your Lab (or any other breed of dog) is fat, it's down to you.

If you see a working Labrador, they'll be lean and muscular, because they need to be faster and more agile, and it's the same with German shepherds who are police dogs. You might liken working dogs to the sporty version of a car model: they basically look the same – and they are pretty much the same – but the bodywork will be streamlined and the engine souped up.

Dogs love food and are motivated by the thought of it (although not all dogs), which is why we use treats as a reward in training. But we only want them to eat what's appropriate, and your dog should know not to eat anything unless explicitly told to do so by you. That's often easier said than done, as with the dog I once worked with who'd pretend he was after something on one side of the kitchen, but when a person ran towards him, he'd bound over to the bin on the other side of the kitchen, knock it over and pilfer some scraps. Smart!

I once met a ten-year-old cockapoo who was intent on eating everything in his path – dog food, human food, anything food, it was all the same to him. As soon as anyone in the family got food out, this dog would go crazy, and he was quick as lightning. It was quite stressful for the family, because they couldn't prepare food or eat in his presence, and they were embarrassed to take him to friends' houses or out for picnics. It didn't help that although they'd tried to tell visitors not to feed him at the dinner table, not everybody obeyed the rules (in my job, it's sometimes about teaching the family self-control as well as the dog!).

When I paid them a visit, I noticed that there were times when there was food around and the dog wasn't going for it – that's when they needed to praise him but were forgetting to do so. I also needed to get the basics right and get the dog to understand the difference between human and dog food.

To do that, whenever he backed away from the table, I'd get up, throw a dog treat into his bowl, which was a couple of metres away from the table, and tell him what a good boy he was (feeding him from the table after telling him to back off would have confused him). We got to the stage where we were putting human food on the floor and he wasn't going for it, because he knew that if he backed off, he was going to get a treat. (I did this not to taunt him, but because in the real world outside the training scenario, occasionally we drop food, and some of it can be poisonous to dogs.) He had a couple of wobbles when we put sausages down, but I stood up, blocked him with my foot, told him to back off and gave him another dog treat. It was all about clarity, which he hadn't had for the first ten years of his life.

I was a bit more apprehensive about taking him over the park, because it's a less controlled environment – and I'd seen a video of him jumping onto a picnic table, where a couple were trying to eat their lunch. So initially I used a 10m line, which gave us a chance to halt him if we needed to, while rewarding him with a bit of sausage for coming back. Things like long lines are similar to stabilisers on a kid's bike – they're great for training but eventually you won't need them.

This dog was probably thinking, 'I really want to raid that picnic over there, but if I hear "wait", I don't have an option but to wait, because I'm on this lead. And if I hear "come", I might as well go back, because I'll get a bit of delicious sausage.' Amazingly, before the day was out, he was holding his ground with a whole picnic right in front of him, which shows that you can teach an older dog new tricks!

Dogs are crafty and fast, so there are always going to be times when they get to food quicker than you. If that happens, don't panic, because it just fuels the fire. What you need in a situation like that – maybe you're having a picnic over the park and your dog has made off with someone else's pork pie – is good recall, first and foremost, and a drop ('out') command that works.

There are dogs who will eat anything – and I'm not just talking about food. It often starts with a dog just wanting something in their mouth, but when they run off with an object that's contraband (the TV remote, spectacles etc.), they soon realise they're being chased by a person, desperate to take it from them. And in order to keep hold of the prize, they start to gobble it down.

The best method to counteract this is to correct the behaviour where it starts. With your dog on a lead, place all sorts of bits and pieces on the floor in front of them, things he'd usually swallow. When he looks like he's about to snatch something, calmly and clearly tell him 'no', then say 'leave' as he moves away. Note the timing here: we're using what will become our word prompt – 'leave' – whilst he is moving away, not before, to make the correct association. Reward him with a treat or, if he's not particularly food motivated, give him an appropriate toy instead. Often dogs that display this type of behaviour aren't actually looking for food but just want to hang on to something. I particularly see it in working breeds like retrievers or spaniels, who were bred to carry things in their mouths. If this is the case for your dog, why not channel their instincts in the right direction? I've even seen people give their dog something like a little blanket that they like to carry around in their mouth – think Linus from the *Peanuts* comic strips.

If your dog is prone to gobbling things outside, then it becomes a case of starting with him on a lead outdoors and walking past the tempting items at a bit of a distance, before graduating to a long line. This way, if your dog were to go to snatch something, you could catch him, again using the 'leave' command and rewarding him for good behaviour. In this situation, the long line acts as a bridge to when you eventually feel confident enough to remove the lead altogether.

However greedy your dog is and however big he gets, rest assured that it's unlikely to ever get close to the heaviest dog that ever lived: Zorba the mastiff, who lived in England, peaked at 330lb in 1989. That's about 24 stone (150kg), or the weight of an upright piano!

Should my dog swim?

Some dogs just seem to love water, while some dogs don't. In fact, there's a great clip doing the rounds on social media that proves exactly that: there are about 30 dogs in a yard, and while half of them are jumping in and out of paddling pools and clearly enjoying being sprayed with hoses, the other half are huddled in the corner, looking on with forlorn expressions on their faces.

Generally, breeds that were designed to hunt or retrieve near water, such as Labradors and Newfoundlands (which were both fishing dogs originally), are going to get on well with the wet stuff. I had a Labrador-boxer rescue, and I'll never forget the first time we took her to the seaside in Devon: I chucked a ball on a rope into the sea and she immediately knew what to do, namely throw herself in, retrieve the ball on a rope from the surf and bring it back to me.

Other obvious water lovers are Spanish and Portuguese water dogs and poodles, which were all bred to retrieve game from water. On a side note, have you ever wondered why poodles are traditionally shaved down to the skin in certain areas? That tight, curly hair they have on their torso insulates their vital organs when plunging into freezing water, while their clipped back ends make them more hydrodynamic (like Olympic swimmers who remove all the hair from their bodies for streamlining). Nowadays, most poodles don't do much swimming in frozen water, so those you see at dog shows, with the pom-pom ankles, are very stylised versions.

Some breeds – the springer spaniel for example – are a bit 50–50: some springers love swimming, some hate it. And be careful with brachycephalic breeds, like pugs and French bulldogs, because they tire easily and struggle to keep their noses above water; and short-legged dogs, like dachshunds and corgis, because they find it difficult to propel themselves.

If you've got a dog that doesn't seem to like water, ask yourself if it's really an issue. Chances are it isn't – if they see water, they just won't go in it, and we probably shouldn't force the issue.

If you do want to teach your dog to swim, don't just drop them in: they'll probably be able to swim, because almost all dogs can, but it will scare the living daylights out of them and they'll never want to go near water again, which will be a bit of a nightmare when it comes to giving them a bath.

Maybe get your dog used to water by taking them somewhere calm and safe, like a lake with a small beach, where they can get their feet wet first. Throw a ball a couple of metres in, and if your dog retrieves it, keep throwing it a bit further each time. Slowly, slowly, slowly. They might only fancy wading in up to their knees or armpits, or they might suddenly realise they like swimming.

One of my Rotties used to wade in and lie down, just out of my reach. That was him cooling down, but he'd do it on a fairly average October day, when I didn't really want to be taking my shoes and socks off and paddling in. He'd look at me as if to say, 'What are you gonna do about it?' and eventually I'd have to bite the bullet.

On the flip side, you get the odd dog who loves water too much, which can be really quite scary for their owners. Dogs seem to have no concept of the danger they might be in in water, and we don't really know how long they can swim for. On top of that, most dogs don't react to recall commands when they're happily paddling around.

I was chatting to a chap the other day who has a springer spaniel, which is a breed that normally loves water. Her name was Ebba (an unusual name, but she came from Sweden, where I understand there's quite a lot of water!) and she was getting on a bit, so her owners were worried she'd swim out too far, get tired and not come back.

The question is, how do you do recall when your dog's out on the water? There's a lot I can do, but I can't walk on water – and neither can my clients! But a key piece of kit would be a long line, a special floating one that can't sink and get caught up in underwater vegetation. You've got the best of both worlds: if you want to let her have a swim you can, but you have the long lead to guide her back in when you need to.

You can also train your dog not to go into the water in the first place with a wait command. When she's hurtling towards the lake, say 'Wait.' If she doesn't, stop her with the long line, and if she does, give her a treat where she stopped. After a while, you'll be able to stop her from going in, and call her to get out of the water without using the line.

Weirdly, some dogs will happily jump into muddy puddles and ponds but as soon as you show them a bath, it's the end of the world. It's the same with children: we know how much kids love splashing about in their wellies, but bath time can be a bit of an ordeal. That's to do with association: dogs and children splash about in puddles of their own free will, while we force them to have baths.

If you do have a dog who isn't keen on bathing, get them used to it bit by bit, maybe by using a flannel to begin with and starting with less sensitive parts of the body, rather than the head. Oh, and use proper dog shampoo, not the smelly stuff you lather yourself with. Because they're worth it!

Why don't our dogs get on?

Sometimes, someone will get in touch with me and say, 'I met someone with a dog, like me, and we thought it would be lovely, but our dogs hate each other.' That can cause real problems in a relationship, and potentially kybosh a new one, because if you can't even visit each other's home, what's the point?

Often in situations like this it gets a bit complicated, because people can be a bit overprotective of their own dog, or even the opposite, in that they're desperate for their dog not to be a nuisance to the other dog. Both people in the early stage of a relationship are desperate to make a good impression on the other and the whole thing becomes super complex.

So how do you get two dogs to be nice to each other and eventually co-habit when they don't entirely see eye to eye? My advice is usually to meet somewhere neutral the first few times, like a local park, because bringing one dog into the other one's domain before they've had time to get to know each other can cause problems. Meeting for the first time between four walls can create a pressure-cooker situation, with one dog thinking, 'Who the hell is this walking through my front door?'

Get the dogs used to walking a few yards apart from each other in straight lines, because it's less confrontational if they're facing in the same direction. Apparently, in Roman times, if a couple of soldiers had an argument in their barracks, instead of settling it with a face-to-face punch-up, they'd go for a walk together along one of their famous straight roads. They'd walk alongside each other while talking things over, and only when they'd sorted things out would they turn around and walk back again. It might sound odd, but I'm told that people worked out their differences quicker that way. There's something about the nature of walking in parallel, as opposed to facing off, that makes the situation less confrontational. I'm sure there's a lesson here we can apply when introducing dogs to each other.

Apply the Roman centurion technique to your dogs and hopefully they will start to take an interest in each other, including sniffing each other's backsides (while that's not OK if teenagers do it, it's perfectly normal for dogs). And when you do decide to go back to one or the other's house, try to sweep through the front door in one continuous motion, so that the dogs are thinking, 'We were having a nice time on that walk, and we're still having a nice time now we're in the house.'

Keep things simple – each person should take responsibility for their own dog (so you've divided the workload). Then from moment to moment, ask yourself whether your dog's behaviour is good. If it is, make sure you remember to praise your dog. If it isn't, make the unwanted behaviour unattractive in an appropriate way. Focus on your own dog, reward the good behaviour (calm, inquisitive, confident) and make sure you don't reward any unwanted behaviour. If you do that, the signals you send out to your dog will be a lot clearer.

Another common scenario people worry about, reasonably enough, is introducing a puppy to a nervous dog. I recently heard about a Border terrier called Hamish who could be quite aggressive and was making it difficult for his owner to socialise with her daughter, who had just got a cavapoo puppy called Teddy. Whenever Teddy came to visit, Hamish would be put in another room, because they were worried about what he might do. The 'never the twain shall meet' policy prevents accidents but of course doesn't get them used to each other.

Often when you've got a dog who's nervous with other dogs, it's as if they keep a list, like a bouncer at the door to a big event: 'Yeah, you're OK. And I'm OK with you. Your name's on the list, come in. But *you*?! There's no way *you're* coming in . . .' It's usually a territory thing, which is why it's always better to meet on neutral ground first, or take the older, nervous dog to the puppy's house, where he doesn't feel like he has to defend anything.

When you do introduce them, be ready for anything, because it's impossible to predict whether two dogs are going to get on or not. I also recommend each owner taking responsibility for their own dog (or designating each person in a couple responsibility for one dog if we're talking about an old dog and new puppy). If you don't and it does kick off, it can quickly descend into a cacophony of instructions, with neither dog knowing who's being told to do what by who. Another idea is to pop a muzzle on the adult dog, not only for the obvious reason, but also because it will allow you to relax a little (and your demeanour rubs off, remember). And, as always, praise them both if and when they back off. Keep that up for a while, and they might end up getting on royally. Even Barney learning to *tolerate* Hugo might be viewed as a success.

Newly introduced dogs often scrap over toys and food, in which case it becomes very much like parenting: if tempers get frayed and things start getting a bit out of hand, someone needs to step in and say, 'Ah, ah, no, we need to share nicely.' It might just be that if one of the dogs goes to steal the other one's toy, you take it off them and don't give it back until he's calmed down. If you're a new couple getting your dogs to meet, that's probably best coming from the thief's owner, at least to start with, for the good of the dog and the relationship! Usually, the dogs will sort things out over time and become best of buddies, just like toddlers.

Occasionally, I hear about two dogs who go from being best buddies to sworn enemies, almost overnight. Sometimes, it's impossible to say why that's happened, but on other occasions there are clues. I once went to see a couple who had a Yorkshire terrier and a rough collie. The guy had the Yorkshire terrier before he moved in with his partner, who owned the rough collie. They got on fine until the rough collie had to have an operation and was in the vet hospital for a week. When she came back everything had changed – the Yorkshire terrier wouldn't accept her back.

Every time they saw each other, these dogs would become extremely aggressive – this wasn't handbags at dawn, they might have done some proper damage – and it put a massive strain on their mum and dad's relationship. To make it even worse, they were understandably protective of the collie, who'd just had an operation.

They ended up having to keep the dogs in separate parts of the house, so that it was like an obstacle course of closed doors. They'd created a routine of opening doors in the right order every time they wanted to let one dog in or one dog out of a room, but that was just perpetuating the problem.

I never look forward to a job that involves two dogs fighting, because it can be really hard to patch things up and make them friends again. It's hard enough with humans, and you can talk to them.

Clearly, the owners needed to make some changes, and my first thought was to try to take the heat out of the situation. To that end, starting training in the back garden seemed to make most sense, because while they were still pretty bad out there, it was less of a pressure cooker than inside the house.

First, I needed to calm the owners down, because their understandable anxiety was rubbing off on the dogs. Then I got the dogs to walk towards each other on their leads, and if they did look like they were about to lose the plot, I stepped in the way. But what had been missing most of all was praise.

The owners had been putting the dogs together and then splitting them up and telling them off, which is perfectly understandable, because fighting dogs can be scary. But they'd been completely forgetting to tell them what good boys they were on the odd occasions they did back down. That's also understand-able, because you don't really feel like telling dogs who have just been fighting what good boys they are! But in order to think dog, you need to think from moment to moment. If what you're looking at is a good moment, you need to let your dog know that, regardless of what happened a minute ago.

Once the dogs tolerated each other, the next stage was to move back into the house. The trick here is to go for a nice walk with them and when you walk back into the house, try to keep that calm energy with you. Then keep the dogs on the lead if necessary, so you can get them used to being in the same room together, and reward them for being calm. Take your time, Rome wasn't built in a day. Be aware that this might take days or weeks, not just minutes. Although you might be pleasantly surprised.

A problem with sharing or resource guarding isn't exclusive to cocker spaniels or cockapoos, but it does crop up quite often with those breeds. Whether it's a ball, a stick or a soft toy, they'll growl, nip and occasionally fight to stop another dog from playing with it. And if they don't want to play any more, nobody's playing.

Sometimes this refusal to share comes down to a dog being a bit bossy with other dogs and wanting everything to happen on their terms, and sometimes that's down to the owner. Let's say you're at home, the dog's telling you he wants to go to the loo, and you open the back door immediately. When he wants to come back in, you let him back in immediately. When he wants food, you give it to him immediately. When he wants you to throw the ball, you throw it immediately. There's a pattern here, isn't there? The upshot is that he's in control of you. Whatever he wants, he asks for and you give it to him – which is the opposite of what my mum used to say to me: '"I want" never gets ...'

If you had a child who was saying 'I want, I want, I want' all the time, you probably wouldn't be so accommodating, because you know you'd end up with a spoilt child – the sort of child who doesn't want to share toys with other children and takes his ball home when he doesn't want to play any more! But because dogs can't speak, are cute and very skilful at deploying their puppy-dog eyes, we end up saying, 'Oh, go on then,' umpteen times a day.

So if you do have a bossy dog who refuses to share, think about all the times your dog tells you what to do and start getting him to play by your rules. So if he wants to go to the toilet and you're doing something else, tell him you're busy and you'll let him out in a minute. If he wants you to throw a ball, tell him you're not going to do it right now, but you might do later when he's not pestering. It's not a case of not doing those things at all, it's a case of doing them on your terms.

In the meantime, be careful not to just stick your hand in when he's barking and growling at other dogs, although you could stand between them. That's you saying, 'Hey, no. I'll take care of this, not you. And I don't care what the other dogs did, you're not allowed to react in that way.' And if he doesn't want to play any more, that's fine. We're always hearing that we have to keep our dogs active, and that is important. But even working breeds that do most things at 100mph like to retreat to their beds and relax every now and again.

I once heard from a lady whose cockapoo didn't want to share with another dog, specifically a puppy who had just been introduced to the house. If the puppy went anywhere near the lady he'd growl and bark or run at the poor little thing, and his behaviour seemed to be escalating, which is never a good situation.

The cockapoo was a male, and his owners wondered if neutering him might solve the problem. That's often the first thing people think of when they've got an aggressive male dog, but it's not a magic wand, and can actually make things worse.

If your male dog is acting out of nervousness, if you then take the testosterone away, some of his bravado will also be extinguished, and he may end up more scared – and therefore more aggressive – than he was before. For that reason, and because you can't glue his testicles back on, you could opt for chemical castration. This is temporary, so you'll be able to see if it has the desired effect, and then you can go down the surgical route if it does. As ever, have a chat with your vet.

In the case of this particular cockapoo, a new star had arrived and taken his limelight. And he'd never had a puppy in the house before, so didn't know how to behave. That said, he was still being a bit of a bully and needed to understand that he wasn't in charge; his owners were. They were the ones who'd brought the puppy into the house, so now they needed to be saying to their adult dog, 'We've said it's OK, so you need to jolly well back off.'

Famously, if a bully's behaviour reaps rewards, their bullying will get worse, which is why you don't want to take the puppy away from him. Instead, if he starts kicking off, get between him and the puppy, stand your ground and tell him, calmly and assertively, no. If you're a bit anxious, one of you could have him on his lead, while the other one does the talking (and it goes without saying that they should be supervised at all times). Slowly but surely, he should get used to the puppy being in the same room as him. 'Share nicely!' is effectively what we're saying here. It's not so different to parenting, is it?

Do dogs and humans fall out?

Earlier in the book I explained how dogs aren't known to hold grudges like we do. The problem is humans, many of whom hold grudges as an inbuilt design fault.

If a dog does something naughty, like wee on the sofa while you're out, that moment is over as far as that dog is concerned. But you might come home, see what he's done and decide not to speak to him for hours. The dog will be thinking, 'What's his problem? Why is he being all weird?' and maybe become withdrawn. That's when we might start thinking, 'What's up with the dog?' You could end up with a situation where you don't interact with each other for ages, so somebody has to be the grown-up, and it's probably best if it's you.

The problem is that there's great potential here for things to go downhill. Sometimes people resent the fact that the dog isn't interacting with them, while other people feel upset that their dog who used to love them doesn't seem to now, or perhaps even feel their dog dislikes them. Emotions can cloud the issue, so the important thing is to try to see things clearly and think with your head, not your heart. Another thing we do that makes things worse is we often try too hard to win back a dog's affection, so we approach them all the time and try to force the issue. You end up in the role of an unwanted suitor: the more you try, the worse you make it. You have to give the dog time to come back and rediscover that you're a great person to be with. In general terms this isn't about doing, it's more about being. For some of us, it's hard to be more passive, less active (being less active is certainly not in my nature either), but sometimes you have to accept that patience is a virtue and give the dog a chance to approach you and reward the good behaviours.

One sad story involved a guy and his partner's parents' Labrador. For years, this man and the Labrador had got on fine. But for reasons unknown, the Labrador suddenly started regarding the man with great suspicion. When the guy visited, the dog would run straight upstairs or hide under the table and stay there until he left. From under the table, the dog would give the man sideways glances, a sure sign of fear.

They tried to mend bridges with treats (usually a good bet with Labradors!), but once she'd scoffed a treat, she'd run away again. The harder he tried to get the Labrador to love him, the worse it was becoming. The guy felt awful that this dog, who to all appearances used to love him and who was OK with everybody else, seemed to be scared of him. But while there probably was a trigger, there was no point in dwelling on it, because he couldn't go back in time and fix it. And dogs are very good at living in the moment – nobody ever sent a dog on a mindfulness course.

The best bet in that situation isn't to go after her rattling a bag of treats, because that could just scare her even more. Being a Labrador, she'll probably take the treat, but that doesn't mean she's happy. Instead, just hang around and wait for the dog to approach you. Maybe follow your partner into the room and sit down (sitting down makes you look less imposing to a dog) and if she comes towards you, get your partner to praise her and drop her a treat in the first couple of instances. That's sending a clear message that if you're brave and inquisitive, you'll be rewarded, instead of being ignored under the table. Then you start to praise and give her the odd treat, initially without making eye contact. Let her have a sniff and don't rush into stroking her. Break things down into baby steps and soon, you'll hopefully be on good terms again.

On the subject of dogs who listen to one owner and not the other, there's no rule that says one person has to do all the training. In fact, one person doing everything and the other person doing nothing is the road to ruin, because your dog will probably end up respecting the trainer and not the shirker.

I once did a one-on-one consultation with a lady who was a child psychologist, which was fascinating for me, because we spent a lot of time discussing the similarities between child–human and dog–human relationships.

This lady said she was always telling parents that the way you teach rules, for example what is good behaviour and what is bad behaviour, isn't so important; what's important is that both parents know what the rules are and apply them consistently, even if both have different styles, voices, mannerisms and so forth. In other words, it's the principles that count, and you don't have to become mirror-images of each other to be teaching the same things. And it's exactly the same with dogs.

Maybe make a list of the dog's house rules and stick them on the fridge, at least in the early stages. I don't mean to patronise people, but it's a good way to make sure you're singing from the same hymn sheet.

When it can become a real problem is if you start a relationship with someone else whose dog is out of control, especially if that dog is coming into your house, chewing furniture, jumping up at visitors and doing its business on the carpet. If that's the case, I'd advise against saying, 'Your dog did this, your dog did that,' because that's likely to drive a wedge between you. Instead, explain to your partner that their dog's bad behaviour is creating problems in the relationship and that you should both make an effort to train him. I realise I've slipped into relationship counselling with that bit of advice, but if you and your partner are at odds, the chances of your dog's behaviour improving are considerably reduced.

Back in the 1970s, an American psychologist called Edward Tronick did a famous experiment called the Still Face Paradigm (SFP). Before the SFP, it was widely believed that babies didn't interact with their mums or dads in meaningful ways – in other words, it didn't matter how you looked at your baby, because they didn't know what any of your expressions meant. But Tronick showed that wasn't the case, and that babies actually hated expressionless faces.

Tronick's original set-up was pretty crude. He sat babies in a seat facing their mums, who started out by chatting and smiling, while making eye contact. The babies responded by vocalising, smiling back and pointing. When the mum turned away and turned back again, this time with a still, unsmiling face, the baby did everything she was doing previously, but the mum's face remain unmoved. Within a few seconds, the baby began to get upset, looking away, waving her arms around and wailing. At that point, the mum relaxed her face and started interacting with the baby again, which quickly repaired the connection. The SFP has been tweaked many times over the years, and it's been discovered that an adult's still face increases a baby's heartrate.

I mention the SFP experiment because it was tried out on dogs in 2021, by scientists from Argentina and Spain, and the results were much the same. They found that dogs showed a two-thirds reduction in the number of attempts to make eye contact if a person looked at them with a still face. On top of that, physical contact initiated by the dog went down by more than a half. In other words, if you're expressive with your dogs, they're more likely to think you're having a meaningful social interaction.

Bear this in mind if you've fallen out with your dog, especially if you've got a naturally expressionless face. You might think you're apologising and repairing the relationship, but your dog might be thinking, 'Fair enough, be like that,' and things can spiral downwards. One sad evening, you're slouched on the sofa thinking, 'This dog doesn't love me any more,' and your dog's lying in his bed, looking up at you and thinking, 'I don't think this person loves me any more.' And next thing you know, people will be talking about you down the pub:

'How's John and his dog?'

'Oh, didn't you hear? They're not speaking . . .'

Is my dog unfixable?

I have to be honest, one question that often crosses my mind but never passes my lips is, 'Why did you get this dog in the first place?'

I might be standing in a small house, looking at an out-of-control Great Dane, and the owner will say, 'It's the dog I always wanted.' I'll be thinking, 'I always wanted an articulated lorry, but it didn't fit on my drive.'

But when you're a dog trainer, you can't just say, 'I've got the answer to all your problems – a Labrador,' you just have to work with what the owner has. One of those things is genetics, which dictate appearance and certain behaviours, another is everything the dog has learnt in its life so far. I often end up saying to people, 'I know you've said you've not trained this dog, but you have, you just don't know it.' Everything you do in front of your dog sends out signals, whether you're aware of it or not.

A question I'm often asked is, 'Do you ever fail to fix a dog?' The answer to that is yes. It's rare, less than one in a hundred, but sometimes I have to break out the phrase, 'This isn't a match made in heaven.'

Let's say you've a dog that's got a history of biting people, doesn't like strangers coming in, doesn't like children, and now you're pregnant. It might be best to rehome that dog, not only for the safety of your baby, but also because that dog is going to have a better life with somebody else, where they can have everything they need and all the attention that they want.

Is my dog still happy?

It's important to say that you should never write a disabled dog off too quickly.

Recently, a friend of mine's young dog got attacked and had her tongue bitten off. I worried she would have to be put down – how would she drink or cool herself by panting? – but when I spoke to her owner a week or so later, she told me she'd quickly worked out how to bite or scoop water from her bowl. As time went on, she found other ways to keep cool. And while she couldn't give her owner licks, she'd sniff her eyes instead. Her endearing new behaviour actually made her very special to her owner.

Dogs are brilliant at adapting, especially those who are disabled from birth or have an accident as a puppy. I once met a three-legged whippet who lost one of his front legs in a nasty accident. You'd expect him to have slowed down after that, but he pulled like crazy on the lead and wasn't much slower than his four-legged whippet mates when off it. The only thing I needed to teach him was how to walk nicely on a lead, and he learnt as fast as any other dog.

In most cases, it seems like a front leg is less of a life-changer than a back leg, because most of a dog's power comes from the rear end. Then again, you see dogs with wheels attached to the back end, usually because they've suffered a spinal injury. Dogs on wheels benefit from a lot of attention from strangers, which is nice, but not all dogs take to wheels so well (big dogs missing rear limbs can struggle, because it puts an awful lot of stress on the front ones).

I also worked with a puppy who was expected to be a guide dog, but unfortunately was born blind herself. But she still made a great pet. She used her incredible hearing to follow footsteps, and after a couple of hours of training, she was walking to heel in her owner's garden, even when I put a few twists and turns in. As with Tripod the whippet, her disability wasn't a problem – in fact to her it was barely a disability at all!

Dogs are usually more relaxed about their supposed disabilities than their owners. It's almost as if they wake up from a leg amputation and think, 'Oh, this is different. How does it work?' Then they'll take a few ginger steps and think, 'I reckon I could get used to this. After all, I've still got three legs.'

I recently spoke to a dog ophthalmologist and, being a medical woman, she was very logical. If she saw a dog who was blind in one eye, she'd say to the owner, 'Well, the eye is blind, it's never going to see again. Also, your dog is in some discomfort, and there's a high chance this will develop into glaucoma, which would be extremely painful. So I recommend removing the eye.'

She didn't want to be removing any eyes, it's the last thing an eye specialist wants to do, but the logic is often too clear to ignore. Of course, it's a much more difficult decision, and can be very traumatic, for many owners. That said, I was told that most of them understood that they needed to let their head rule their heart and allow the ophthalmologist to do her thing.

As I mentioned earlier, of our three dogs, Scooby the boxer is deaf and Tish the Patterdale is blind, but there are ways of making their lives easier.

We make sure not to move furniture around and we take Tish to an enclosed dog field, where she can run around with a load of other dogs without worrying about getting lost. She seems to detect where my other two dogs are without any problems (although she's stopped nipping big boy Scooby to put him in his place, not because of my training skills, but because she can't see him properly), and if I want her to follow me, I walk up to her and say, 'I'm here, baby,' before giving her a little tickle. I think she smells my trouser leg, but however she does it, she stays right with me. As for Scooby, he doesn't have any recall if he's not looking our way, but he understands what we're saying through our hands.

I've seen videos of deaf and blind dogs who are still happily going about their life. As long as a dog can move around and is pain-free, I say let them get on with it. Dogs don't want humans to stop them doing stuff. They just want to be treated as normal and for their owners to focus on what they can do, rather than what they can't.

Vets are always talking about 'quality of life'; that's what it always comes back to. So when they suggest that your dog's leg, for example, might have to be amputated, they're doing so in the knowledge that your dog will almost certainly cope. At the same time, there are lots of ethical considerations when it comes to deciding whether your dog is beyond help or not.

Most vets will also tell you that amputation is a better bet than experimental surgery that might not work and will cost you a fortune (it might sound callous talking about money in relation to your dog's health, but it's the reality for most people). If experimental surgery is an option, ask yourself who you'd be doing it for, you or the dog? It might be the case that you've got more of an emotional attachment to the injured leg, let's say, than your dog. There are rarely absolute right or wrong answers in cases like these, but my advice is always to make the decision for the dog's good, thinking about their quality of life. Your emotions come second, I'm afraid.

I've spoken to veterinary oncologists about chemotherapy for dogs, and they tell me treatments aren't as extreme for dogs, because, unlike with a human patient, they can't have that difficult conversation: 'There are two ways of doing this. We can go easier on you, but there's a chance it won't be as effective. Or we can do the opposite: you'll feel really ill, but you'll have a better chance of recovery.' Because a dog doesn't know what's happening to them, it's just assumed that they would choose the route of feeling less ill.

Dogs can also have blood transfusions, which is an ethical dilemma for some people, because dogs obviously can't consent to having blood removed from them. My personal feeling is that if the transfusion process doesn't harm the healthy dog and saves a sick dog's life (in fact one donation can save a number of dogs' lives), then surely it's OK. However, having seen a doggy blood transfusion, something I do know is that instead of a digestive biscuit and a cup of tea afterwards, the brave dog donor gets a treat and a bucket-load of love from all the nurses as a reward.

Thinking of getting a rescue? Don't rule out a dog with a disability, because while four legs are good, you might hit it off with a three- or even two-legged dog even better.

Epilogue

As I've already outlined, we'll never know how dogs became our best friends, all those thousands of years ago. But like a lot of great love stories, there's a good chance that our relationship was tempestuous at the beginning, when dogs were still wolves. Humans were likely bitten or mauled or even killed in those early encounters. But at some point, tempestuousness would have given way to tolerance.

Those early human domesticators didn't befriend wolves out of any sense of affection. Wolves were simply useful to have around the place, guarding as they did against predators. Wolves probably felt much the same. Why use up all that energy hunting when you could hang around on the fringes of a human camp and get a free meal? Pretty smart, if you ask me.

You can imagine that practicality skipped to a mild sense of affection when the odd tame wolf decided to stand its ground – maybe even come a bit closer – when people approached, rather than run. Then when wolves morphed into proto-dogs, and started travelling and hunting alongside humans, that mild sense of affection grew into something stronger.

By at least 14,000 years ago, people loved their dogs enough to be buried alongside them, as proved by the Bonn-Oberkassel dog in Germany, which most experts agree was deliberately interred with a man and a woman.

A lot of water has flowed under the bridge since the Bonn-Oberkassel dog passed on to the great kennel in the sky, but while humans have been busy conquering the world, and often making a mess of things, dogs have never left our side (not that I'm saying dogs are complicit in our mistakes!). As a result, dogs have come to rely on us for their very survival, while humans have moulded dogs to fit ever more perfectly into our world.

Elvis Costello once sang, 'What's so funny 'bout peace, love and understanding?' Nothing much, because if you don't understand your dog, peace might be in short supply – and the feeling of love might prove elusive.

Luckily, all those years spent in each other's company mean my job as a dog trainer is often just a case of tweaking and facilitating. And it's why you should never abandon hope that you and your dog will one day be singing the same tunes (metaphorically, of course – I'm not a miracle worker!).

Maybe I haven't managed to convince you 100 per cent that your dog loves you, but I hope you at least know your dog better than you did at the start of this book. Maybe you feel your bond is even tighter than it was.

So ... the big question. Does your dog love you? Well, you care enough about them to have bought this book and made it to the end, so you're clearly a dog lover. Do they love you back in turn? Course they do!

Acknowledgements

Oh, where do I start with acknowledgements? I'm not going to name anyone specifically because I'm bound to forget someone and kick myself from now to eternity.

It takes many people to put a book together and I want to say a huge thank you to everyone at Penguin and my agents M&C Saatchi Merlin for being there every step of the way and helping bring this book to you. Like TV production, publishing is a team game.

I'm always reflecting how lucky I am to be doing a job I love, meeting amazing dogs and their people, doing my best to help both groups along the way. Without all those experiences and all of the learning it provided this wouldn't be much of a book, and so I'd like to thank everyone who has invited me into their lives along the way.

Let's not forget that behind most authors is a person shouting 'Your tea's going cold' up the stairs. I owe a large debt of gratitude to my partner Nikki for being so supportive and inspirational throughout. (I realise I said I wouldn't name people, but rules/exceptions and all that ...)

Finally … drum roll … thank YOU, dear reader, for buying/ lending/stealing my book. I have three dogs and a custard cream habit to support don' cha know. I hope you liked it.

List of Sources

Prologue

Chabba, Seerat, 'Dogs Prefer Owner's Praise to Food, New Study Finds', *International Business Times*, 29 August 2016, www.ibtimes.com/dogs-prefer-owners-praise-food-new-study-finds-2408484

Coren, Stanley, 'Canine Empathy: Your Dog Really Does Care If You Are Unhappy', *Psychology Today*, 7 June 2012, www.psychologytoday.com/us/blog/canine-corner/201206/canine-empathy-your-dog-really-does-care-if-you-are-unhappy

Grimm, David, 'How dogs stole our hearts: Canines make humans produce more "trust hormone," and vice versa', *Science*, 16 April 2015, www.science.org/content/article/how-dogs-stole-our-hearts

Chapter 1 – How Human Are Dogs?

Andersson, Jasmine, 'Dogs can cry when owners come home', BBC News, 23 August 2022, www.bbc.co.uk/news/science-environment-62645859

Arnold, Carrie, '"Puppy dog eyes" evolved so dogs could communicate with us', *National Geographic*, 17 June 2019, www.nationalgeographic.com/animals/article/dogs-eyebrows-humans-communication

Clark, Carol, 'Emory neuroscientist explores "What It's Like to Be a Dog"', Emory University News Center, 7 September 2017, news.emory.edu/stories/2017/09/esc_berns_dogs_book/campus.html

Coren, Stanley, 'Do Dogs Grieve Over the Loss of an Animal Companion?', *Psychology Today*, 10 November 2016, www.psychologytoday.com/us/blog/canine-corner/201611/do-dogs-grieve-over-the-loss-animal-companion

Evans, Kate, 'Jealous Dogs', *New Zealand Geographic*, May–June 2021, www.nzgeo.com/stories/jealous-dogs/

Hepper, Peter G., 'Long-term retention of kinship recognition established during infancy in the domestic dog', *Behavioural Processes*, Vol. 33, Issues 1–2: 3–14, December 1994, www.sciencedirect.com/science/article/abs/pii/0376635794900566

Horgan, Richard, 'Spooked By Fireworks In Texas, TV Journalist's Beloved Dog Found 7 Years Later . . . In Florida', *Knewz*, 15 December 2022, knewz.com/florida-dog-jazzy/

Merola, Isabella, Prato-Previde, Emanuela and Marshall-Pescini, Sarah, 'Dogs' Social Referencing towards Owners and Strangers', *PLOS One*, 11 October 2012, https://doi.org/10.1371/journal.pone.0047653

Morris, Sophie, 'Dogs get depression too – and they'll need more than walkies to make them feel better', *iNews*, 10 March 2022, inews.co.uk/inews-lifestyle/wellbeing/dogs-get-depression-too-and-theyll-need-more-than-walkies-to-make-them-feel-better-1507886

Owen, James, 'Many Animals – Including Your Dog – May Have Horrible Short-Term Memories', *National Geographic*, 26 February 2015, www.nationalgeographic.com/animals/article/150225-dogs-memories-animals-chimpanzees-science-mind-psychology

Pappas, Stephanie, 'What Do Dogs Dream About?', *Live Science*, 17 February 2016, www.livescience.com/53743-dog-dreams.html

'Stolen dogs reunited with owner after three years', BBC News, 29 November 2022, www.bbc.co.uk/news/uk-england-berkshire-63792256

Yeager, Ashley, 'These genes may be why dogs are so friendly', *Science News*, 19 July 2017, www.sciencenews.org/article/these-genes-may-be-why-dogs-are-so-friendly

Chapter 2 – Can Dogs Read Our Minds?

Albuquerque, Natalia; Guo, Kun; Wilkinson, Anna; Resende, Briseida; Mills, Daniel S., 'Mouth-licking by dogs as a response to emotional stimuli', *Behavioural Processes*, Vol. 146, 42–45, January 2018, www.sciencedirect.com/science/article/abs/pii/S0376635717303005

Colino, Stacey, 'Yes, dogs can "catch" their owners' emotions', *National Geographic*, 4 October 2021, www.nationalgeographic.co.uk/animals/2021/10/yes-dogs-can-catch-their-owners-emotions

Coren, Stanley, 'Dogs Smell Your Emotional State and It Affects Their Mood', *Psychology Today*, 25 October 2017, www.psychologytoday.com/us/blog/canine-corner/201710/dogs-smell-your-emotional-state-and-it-affects-their-mood

Coren, Stanley, 'Study: Dogs Can Identify Liars, and They Don't Trust Them', *Psychology Today*, 24 February 2015, www.psychologytoday.com/us/blog/canine-corner/201502/study-dogs-can-identify-liars-and-they-dont-trust-them

Fugazza, Claudia; Moesta, Alexandra; Pogany, Akos; Miklosi, Adam, 'Social learning from conspecifics and humans in dog puppies', *Scientific Reports*, 8, 9257, 5 July 2018, www.nature.com/articles/s41598-018-27654-0

Vetmeduni, 'No easy judgments: How dogs and wolves judge people', University of Veterinary Medicine, Vienna, 17 August 2022, www.vetmeduni.ac.at/en/universitaet/infoservice/presseinformationen-2022/no-easy-judgments-how-dogs-and-wolves-judge-people

Chapter 3 – Relationship Counselling for Dogs and People

Andics, A.; Gabor, A.; Gacsi, M.; Farago, T.; Szabo, D.; Miklosi, A., 'Neural mechanisms for lexical processing in dogs', *Science*, Vol. 353, Issue 6303, 1030–1032, 30 August 2016, www.science.org/doi/10.1126/science.aaf3777

Hediger, Karin; Turner, Dennis C., 'Can dogs increase children's attention and concentration performance? A randomised controlled trial', *Human–Animal Interaction Bulletin*, Vol. 2, No. 2, 21–39, December 2014, www.researchgate.net/publication/286190655_Can_Dogs_increase_children's_attention_and_concentration_performance_A_randomised_controlled_trial/link/5666b69108ae418a786f510f/download

'New Research says Pet-Owning Children Spend Significantly More Time at School', University of Warwick, 13 June

2002, warwick.ac.uk/newsandevents/pressreleases/ne
100000008349/

Nied, Jennifer, 'Science explains why dogs and their owners
look alike', Simplemost, 19 March 2018, www.simplemost.
com/science-explains-dogs-owners-look-alike/

Oakes, Kelly, 'How pets give your kids a brain boost', BBC
Future, 14 June 2022, www.bbc.com/future/article/
20220609-do-pets-help-childrens-development

Omar, Mohamed, 'Hugging Your Dog Is Making It Stressed
Out, Study Finds', *Huffington Post*, 27 April 2016, www.
huffingtonpost.co.uk/entry/canine-behaviourist-stanley-
coren-explains-why-you-should-not-hug-dogs_uk_571f
822ce4b0a1e971ca8402

Sampathkumar, Mythili, 'Living with dogs can help protect
babies from range of illnesses like asthma', *Independent*, 12
June 2017, www.independent.co.uk/news/world/americas/
dogs-health-asthma-benefits-living-with-pets-babies-children-
illnesses-bacteria-a7786886.html

Wenden, Elizabeth J.; Lester, Leanne; Zubrick, Stephen R.; Ng,
Michelle; Christian, Hayley E., 'The relationship between dog
ownership, dog play, family dog walking, and pre-schooler
social–emotional development: findings from the PLAYCE
observational study', *Pediatric Research*, Vol. 89, 1013–1019, 6
July 2020, www.nature.com/articles/s41390-020-1007-2

Chapter 4 – How Dogs Perceive the World

Coren, Stanley, 'Can Dogs Smell Time?', *Psychology Today*, 22
November 2019, www.psychologytoday.com/us/blog/canine-
corner/201911/can-dogs-smell-time

'Deaf dog Rocco taught to understand sign language', BBC News, 21 January 2022, www.bbc.com/news/uk-wales-60088102

'How to Calculate Dog Years to Human Years', American Kennel Club, 20 November 2019, www.akc.org/expert-advice/health/how-to-calculate-dog-years-to-human-years/

McCaffrey, Julie, 'Meet eight intrepid pets who embarked on incredible journeys – from two to 2,000 miles', *Mirror*, 26 April 2016, www.mirror.co.uk/news/weird-news/might-eight-intrepid-pets-who-7841623

Meyers-Manor, Julia E.; Botten, Marijo L., 'A shoulder to cry on: Heart rate variability and empathetic behavioral responses to crying and laughing in dogs', *Canadian Journal of Experimental Psychology*, Vol. 74, 235–243, September 2020, pubmed.ncbi.nlm.nih.gov/33090854/

Morelle, Rebecca, 'Dogs' brain scans reveal vocal responses', BBC News, 21 February 2014, www.bbc.com/news/science-environment-26276660

Morris, Amanda, 'Yes, your pet can tell time', *Northwestern Now*, 23 October 2018, news.northwestern.edu/stories/2018/october/yes-your-pet-can-tell-time/

Murez, Cara, 'Dogs Can Tell When You're Talking to Them, and Might Prefer Female Voices', *US News*, 24 August 2023, www.usnews.com/news/health-news/articles/2023-08-24/dogs-can-tell-when-youre-talking-to-them-and-might-prefer-female-voices

Pendry, Patricia; Vandagriff, Jaymie L., 'Stress reduction benefits from petting dogs, cats', *American Educational*

Research Association, 15 July 2019, www.sciencedaily.com/
releases/2019/07/190715114302.htm

Sample, Ian, 'Dogs are either optimists or pessimists, claim
scientists', *Guardian*, 11 October 2010, www.theguardian.
com/science/2010/oct/11/dogs-optimists-pessimists

Scott, Ellen, 'Apparently, dogs can smell the time' *Metro*, 6
October 2016, metro.co.uk/2016/10/06/apparently-dogs-can-
smell-the-time-6176025/

Thomson, Jessica E.; Hall, Sophie S.; Mills, Daniel S.,
'Evaluation of the relationship between cats and dogs living
in the same home', *Journal of Veterinary Behavior*, Vol. 27, 35–40,
September–October 2018, www.sciencedirect.com/science/
article/abs/pii/S1558787817302393

Yirka, Bob, 'Dogs may use Earth's magnetic field to navigate',
Phys.org, 20 July 2020, phys.org/news/2020-07-dogs-earth-
magnetic-field.html

Yong, Ed, 'A New Origin Story for Dogs', *The Atlantic*, 2 June
2016, www.theatlantic.com/science/archive/2016/06/the-
origin-of-dogs/484976/

Chapter 5 – Why Do Dogs . . . ?
Whitehead, Michael; Evershed, Nick, 'Interactive: see how your
favourite dog breeds are related to each other', *Guardian*, 24
October 2020, www.theguardian.com/news/datablog/ng-
interactive/2020/oct/25/interactive-see-how-your-favourite-
dog-breeds-are-related-to-each-other

Wrenn, Eddie, 'Man's TRUE best friend: How dogs can
respond to our emotions more than other humans', *Daily
Mail*, 4 September 2012, www.dailymail.co.uk/sciencetech/

article-2198070/Mans-TRUE-best-friend-Dogs-really-console--treat-strangers-just-empathy.html

Chapter 6 – Different Dogs

Cavalli, C.; Dzik, M. V.; Barrera, G.; Bentosela, M., 'Still-face effect in domestic dogs: comparing untrained with trained and animal assisted interventions dogs', *Learning & Behavior*, 5 July 2023, link.springer.com/article/10.3758/s13420-023-00589-x#citeas

Raffan, Eleanor *et al.*, 'Genetic variant may help explain why Labradors are prone to obesity', *Cell Metabolism*, Vol. 23, Issue 5, 893–900, 10 May 2016, https://www.cam.ac.uk/research/news/genetic-variant-may-help-explain-why-labradors-are-prone-to-obesity